Imam Ahmad ibn Hanbal:

'O Son, can there ever be anyone who believes in Allah and (still) has Yazeed as a friend? And why should I not curse the one whom Allah has cursed in His book'

(As Sawaaiq ul Muharriqa of Imam Ibn Hajar Al Haytami)

THE BLESSED IMAM &
THE WRETCHED YAZEED

AN ANALYSIS OF THE TWO CHARACTERS
IN THE TRAGEDY OF KARBALA

ALLAAMA MUHAMMAD SHAFEE OKAARVI

Compiled and Translated by
Muhammad Sajid Younus

THE BLESSED IMAM AND THE WRETCHED YAZEED
An Analysis of the two characters in the tragedy of Karbala

Author: Allaama Muhammad Shafee Okaarvi
Translated by: Muhammad Sajid Younus

Published by: TrueIslam Publications

Website: www.trueislam.org.uk
Email: bookshop@trueislam.org.uk

Published in December 2011 / Muharram 1433
ISBN: 978-0-9568965-3-7

A CIP catalogue record for this book is available with the British Library

Design,Typeset and print
WHITE CANVAS DESIGN
saqib.hussain@whitecanvas.co.uk

CONTENTS

TRANSLATOR'S INTRODUCTION

After the martyrdom of Syeduna Imam Ali, the last of the Khulafa ur Raashideen, there were rival claims to the Caliphate from the Prophet's 🌸 companion Syeduna Ameer Muaawiya and the Prophet's 🌸 grandson Imam Hassan. The two eventually reached a reconciliation and agreed that Ameer Muaawiya becomes the Imam of the Muslims. After Ameer Muaawiya's death his son Yazeed claimed the Caliphate and sought bai'a (pledges of allegiances) from the Umma and even though most reluctantly accepted the leading figures of the Islamic World, especially those residing in Makkah and Madinah, refused. The most prominent and important of them was Imam Husayn, the other grandson of the Prophet 🌸. Yazeed in particular needed his acceptance to achieve legitimacy but Imam Husayn refused as his high and elevated spiritual status within the Umma could not allow him to approve a corrupt and oppressive man like Yazeed for it would have set a precedent that would have destroyed future Islamic societies. Yazeed continued to pressurise Imam Husayn to the extent that he was forced to leave Madeenah for the sanctuary of Makkah. However he was still pressurised there, whilst at the same time the people of Iraq, in particular Kufa, were constantly sending him messages and messengers claiming that they did not accept Yazeed and did not want to. Instead they supported him and wanted him to be their ruler and promised to protect him from Yazeed. When Imam Husayn sent his cousin, Muslim bin Aqeel, to Kufa to determine the situation and he reported back favourably Imam Husayn felt he had no option but to leave Makkah for Kufa, thus tragically, as pilgrims were entering the city for Hajj he had to leave the city of Allah and his forefathers.

However Yazeed had also noticed the emergence of a rival power base in Kufa and ordered his governors, through force or bribery, to bring the people of Kufa to disown Imam Husayn and pledge allegiance to Yazeed. Thus Muslim bin Aqeel was murdered by those who had pledged allegiance to him just a few days earlier and the governor of Kufa then led the very people who had promised to support and protect Imam Husayn to meet up with him en route and surrounded him and his entourage at Karbala. After stopping their food and water for days they mercilessly slaughtered the men and imprisoned the women.

As a result of this massacre the cities of Madeenah and Makkah openly rejected Yazeed who responded by sacking both cities and killing hundreds of the Prophet's 🕌 companions and desecrating the holy masjids.

These vile acts are an undisputed fact of history and have been confirmed by all shades of Islam and as a result the character of Yazeed has been vilified by the Islamic world, some refuse to sully their tongue with him whilst others declare him outside the fold of Islam. However recently, taking advantage of the lack of traditional knowledge amongst the masses, attempts to distort history and present Yazeed in a different light have begun to be made. This well researched book by one of the leading recent day scholars of the subcontinent, Shaykh Muhammad Shafee Okaarvi, better known as Khateeb e Pakistan, provides well reasoned responses, from the Quran, ahadith and statements of the leading scholars, to the misconceptions that are or may come to the surface.

May Allah accept this and keep sound hearts on the true path.

WAS YAZEED A CALIPH
IN TERMS OF SHARIAH?

In light of the rules of Shariah was Yazeed's caliphate legitimate and did all the companions accept his rule?

It is clear that Yazeed's rule was not legitimate and he did not enjoy the unanimous support of the companions. Anyone claiming such a thing would be lying and in contradiction of the events of this great tragedy.

After the passing away of the Prophet ﷺ the Khulafa (Caliphs) of Islam were chosen by the great companions of the time. Although by Yazeed's time many of them had passed away and the bounties of the Prophet's ﷺ time had lifted the children of those great companions were present and many of them had benefitted from the company of the Prophet ﷺ, such as Abdullah bin Umar, Husayn bin Ali, Abdullah bin Zubair and Abdur Rehman bin Abu Bakr. These people epitomised their honourable predecessors and embodied good characteristics and pious deeds, alongwith possessing the ability and acumen for piety, abstention, justice, honesty, integrity, knowledge, wisdom and truth. In the presence of such people it was wholly inappropriate for Yazeed to be put forward as the next Caliph.

The events that led to Yazeed being put forward as Caliph were as follows:

Mugheera bin Shoba was the governor of Kufa and when he found out that Ameer Muaawiya, the Caliph of the time, had decided to remove him from his post he came to Damascus. Here he met with Yazeed and counselled him that most of the Prophet's 🕌 companions had now passed away and only their children remained and he was no less than any of them (to be the next Caliph) and Ameer Muaawiya (his father) should begin requesting people to pledge allegiance to him (i.e. take his bai'a).

Yazeed discussed this matter with his father, who summoned Mugheera to explain himself. Mugheera explained 'You know of the division and bloodshed within the 'Umma after the martyrdom of Syeduna Uthman so it is better to appoint Yazeed in your own lifetime as your heir and avoid similar trouble after you.' Ameer Muaawiya asked 'Who will support me in this?' He assured 'I will look after Kufa and Ziyaad is enough for Basra. After that no one will oppose it.' Ameer Muaawiya ordered him to return to Kufa in his post and discuss the matter with his confidantes.

On his return Mugheera boasted to his friend that he had trapped Ameer Muaawiya in a plot from which there was no escape. Mugheera then paid 30,000 Dirham to ten people of Kufa to go to Damascus and insist upon Ameer Muaawiya appointing Yazeed as his heir and to show him their full support for it. This delegation was led by Mugheera's son Musa. Although Ameer Muaawiya told them not to be hasty he also asked them to remain steadfast upon their opinion and promise.

Afterwards Ameer Muaawiya asked Musa how much his father had paid these people.

Ameer Muaawiya then wrote to Ziyaad, the governor of Basra, and asked him for his views. Ziyaad called Ubayd bin Ka'b and told him that the *Ameer ul Momineen* had sought his views on the matter of making Yazeed his heir but was fearful that people would dislike it and so wanted their support. As Yazeed had many flaws Ziyaad ordered Ubayd to go to Damascus and explain Yazeed's weakness' and advise Ameer Muaawiya to show restraint in this matter and not be hasty.

Ubayd told Ziyaad not to try to oppose Ameer Muaawiya's plan. He suggested that he would instead go and meet with Yazeed and inform him that his father was wishing to seek Bai'a for him and he needed to change to make the matter easy and simple. Ubayd also took a letter from Ziyaad to Ameer Muaawiya asking him not to be hasty and to employ great wisdom and expediency.

In 53 hijri Ziyaad passed away and Ameer Muaawiya decided to start seeking bai'a for Yazeed and began reconciling the leading figures. He sent 100,000 Dirham to Abdullah bin Umar who first accepted, but when he was asked to pledge allegiance to Yazeed he returned the money protesting his Deen was not so cheap.

Ameer Muaawiya then wrote to Marwaan, the governor of Madeenah, and explained that he feared bloodshed within the Muslims after him (over the next Caliph) and to avoid that he wished to appoint the next Caliph during his own lifetime. He ordered him to seek the views of the people of Madeenah; Marwaan gathered all the people together and presented this plan which they all supported in principle but wanted to know who had been chosen as heir. Marwaan relayed this request back to Ameer Muaawiya who revealed that he had chosen Yazeed. Marwaan gathered all the people again in Masjid un Nabawi and revealed 'the Ameer ul Momineen has chosen a very suitable person and has made no mistake in it and his choice is for Yazeed to be the Caliph after him. Verily Allah has given the Ameer great understanding of Yazeed and he has chosen him just as without a doubt Abu Bakr and Umar chose Caliphs too.' Upon this Abdur Rehman bin Abu Bakr rose and protested 'O Marwaan you are wrong and so is Ameer Muaawiya, You do not wish for the betterment of the 'Umma or a selection, you wish to turn the caliphate into a monarchy where one monarch dies his son becomes the next monarch. This is not the practice of Abu Bakr or Umar for they never made any of their children their heirs.' Marwaan ordered for him to be arrested but he escaped to the house of his sister Syeda Aisha. Afterwards Imam Husayn, Abdullah bin Umar and

Abdullah bin Zubair rose and refused to accept Yazeed as the heir. Marwaan informed Ameer Muaawiya of this.

Ameer Muaawiya then sent 100,000 Dirham to Abdur Rehman bin Abi Bakr who refused complaining how he could sell his deen for the duniya?!

At this same time Ameer Muaawiya wrote to the governors of all the regions and ordered them to praise Yazeed in front of the people and make him acceptable to them. He also ordered them to send delegations to Damascus to show support for Yazeed. As a result delegations arrived and praised Yazeed as the most suitable heir to be Caliph. However Muhammad bin Amr bin Hazm arrived from Madeenah and told Ameer Muaawiya that every shepherd will be asked about his flock and he should look carefully at who he was leaving as heir to the matters of the Muslim 'Umma. However the delegations from most of the other regions showed great support for Yazeed.

During all this praise Ahnaf bin Qais was seated quietly. Ameer Muaawiya asked him to speak. He said 'If I speak the truth I fear you people, If I lie I fear God. O Ameer ul Momineen, you are well aware of Yazeed's days and his nights, his hidden and his apparent, his seclusion and his gatherings!'

Over time the people of Iraq and Syria came around to supporting Yazeed but Ameer Muaawiya knew that the people of the Hijaaz would remain an issue. Hijaaz was the heart of Islam and where the great personalities of Islam resided who had integrity and the ability to speak the truth and it was they who could form the greatest opposition. Consequently Ameer Muaawiya headed to Madeenah himself with 1000 cavalrymen and tried to persuade Imam Husayn bin Ali, Abdullah bin Umar al Farooq, Abdullah bin Zubayr, and Abdur Rehman bin Abu Bakr Siddiq by speaking to them harshly. During his stay in the city Ameer Muaawiya paid little heed to these people as they had refused to accept the bai'a of Yazeed. As a result these four left Madeenah for Makkah. Their departure made Ameer Muaawiya's task of convincing the people of Madeenah easier. After the people had accepted Yazeed Ameer Muaawiya complained to Syeda Aisha about the four. However she was well aware of what had happened and complained to Ameer Muaawiya that he had threatened to kill them if they did not accept Yazeed. Ameer Muaawiya asked how he could ever do such a thing for these people's rank was well above that. Syeda Aisha reminded him to be good with them.

Ameer Muaawiya then left for Makka with his companions and met with the people there. He also met these four nobles but this time spoke to them with great respect and love and always sat them at the top of every gathering.

One day Ameer Muaawiya asked the four in seclusion 'Look how good I have been to you and how I have honoured our kinship. Yazeed is your brother and I want you to take his Bai'a.' Abdullah bin Zubair responded 'You have the choice to take one of three ways; do as the Prophet ﷺ did and make no one your heir and the people will choose whoever they wish just as they chose Abu Bakr Siddiq.' Ameer Muaawiya complained 'But there is no one like Abu Bakr today and I fear conflict.' Abdullah bin Zubayr then said 'Ok, then do as Abu Bakr Siddiq did when he appointed Umar al Farooq, who was not even a distant relative, or you can do what Umar al Farooq did and appoint a six man Shura (committee) of people who were neither his relatives or son' Ameer Muaawiya asked 'Do you have anything else to say?' He replied 'No'. Ameer Muaawiya became very angry with them and dissolved the meeting and returned. (Ibn Atheer).

This was how Yazeed came to be the Caliph. As you can see it was not based on the principles of Shariah for it was not unanimously accepted by all the companions or the majority of the Muslims.

Our viewpoint:

Ameer Muaawiya had the best intentions of Islam and the Muslims and based on this wish for their wellbeing he did not want the Muslims to suffer fighting and bloodshed. In light of past events he knew well that if he did not appoint an heir he could not rely on the vision of the Muslims to choose and agree upon a Caliph and there was a possibility that different Caliphs could rise from all the different regions and cause great conflict and bloodshed between the Muslims. He also knew that if he transferred the Caliphate to the Banu Hashim his tribe of the Banu Umayya, which was very proud, would never accept that, especially at a time when it enjoyed great power and resources. He knew that this too would lead to bloodshed amongst the Muslims. This is why he chose Yazeed over people who were more worthy than him. Whether he did right or wrong he did it in the best interests of Islam and the Muslim 'Umma. His supplication (dua) at the time of appointing Yazeed his heir testifies to this 'O Allah, You know that if I appointed Yazeed heir because of the ability I see in him then complete his caliphate and if I did so out of love for him then leave it incomplete' (Al Bidaaya wa Nihaaya)

There is no doubt that Yazeed was well versed in politics and that is why his father chose him as heir over the rest of the Banu Umayya. There is also no doubt that Ameer Muaawiya could never have envisaged the destruction and oppression that Yazeed would commit as his heir. He had specifically bequeathed him about Imam Husayn, that 'he was the Prophet's 鬱 grandson, beloved and because of this most close of relationships had the right to be treated kindly. If the people of Iraq put him up against you, and I am sure they will, and if you overcome him then even then pardon him and remember (his) the relationship with the Prophet 鬱.'

However this wretch disregarded his father's bequest and intoxicated in power committed atrocities that no believer could ever imagine.

Despite this, we cannot have any doubts in the veracity of Ameer Muaawiya for his Companionship of the Prophet 鬱 is a universal fact and this prevents us doubting his veracity.

THE RIGHT TO STAND AGAINST YAZEED

Did Imam Husayn needlessly rebel and cause discord and bloodshed,
which was tantamount to war against Allah and His Prophet ﷺ*?*

In light of the facts only a person suffering from hypocrisy and malice
for the Ahl ul Bait could claim such a thing. Not only that, in reality,
saying such a thing is clear transgression and ignorance.

Obeying Yazeed was not compulsory upon Imam Husayn for he
believed that under the rules of Shariah Yazeed was not worthy of
leading the Muslims. Furthermore Yazeed's caliphate had not been
unanimously established in line with the Shariah and Imam Husayn
had neither taken his bai'a (pledge of allegiance).

Allah states in the Quran: *{And remember that Abraham was tried*
by his Lord with certain commands, which he fulfilled: He said: "I will
make thee an Imam to the Nations." He pleaded: "And also (Imams)
from my offspring!" He answered: "But My Promise is not within the
reach of evil-doers} (2:124)

In explaining this verse the scholars of the 'Umma have clearly
stated that the oppressive, unjust, faasiq and faajir is not worthy of
the Imamate or Caliphate of the 'Umma and the Caliphate of such a
person would be invalid and void.

Allaama Qurtubi writes:

'Verily the Imam will, alongside having the power to establish government, be a man of *ad'l* (justice), *Ihsaan* (benevolence) and *fadh*l (virtue). This is the Imam about whom the Prophet ﷺ said 'Beware not to fight against the rule of the worthy.' As for the *ahl ul fusooq* (transgressors) they are not worthy of it (Imamate).' (Tafseer Qurtubi)

The famous jurist Imam Abu Bakr Al Jassaas Al Hanafee writes under this same verse:

'Thus it is not permissible for a Dhaalim (tyrant) to become a prophet ﷺ or a caliph of a prophet ﷺ, nor become a judge or hold any other position which the people are required to obey in matters of the deen, such as a mufti, witness or narrator of the Prophet's ﷺ hadith.' (Ahkaam ul Quran)

He then writes further on:

'Thus this verse is evidence for the invalidity of the Imamate of a faasiq. Undoubtedly he cannot become a caliph. If a faasiq did ever take up such a position by force it will not be incumbent upon the people to obey or follow him.' (Ahkaam ul Quran)

Imam Raazi writes under this same verse:

'The great majority of jurists and theologians *(mutakallimin)* stipulate the impermissibility of a faasiq becoming an Imam. However there is a difference of opinion about the Imam who becomes faasiq after taking the position of Imam; is his Imamate still valid or not? The majority have inferred from this verse that a faassiq does not have the ability (to continue as Imam).' (Tafseer Kabeer)

Allaama Qaadhi Thanaa ullah Paani Patti writes:

'We state that the meaning of Allah's statement 'But My Promise is not within the reach of evil-doers 'is that if a faasiq becomes an Ameer it is not permissible to obey him in oppression or sin, for the Prophet 鑫 said 'The creation is not to obey in the disobedience of the Creator.' (Tafseer Mazhari)

The Tafseer of this verse of the Quran and the commentaries of the mufassireen prove that the faasiq, faajir, oppressive and tyrannical are not worthy of the Imamate or Caliphate and such an Imamate or Caliphate would be invalid and following and obeying him impermissible.

Verse 2:

Allah states: {*And do not obey the order of the transgressors Who cause corruption in the land and do not amend*} (Quran 26:151-152)

This verse also proves that the transgressing rulers should not be obeyed, those who through kufr, shirk, oppression or fisq spread discord in the nation and do not correct the nation through belief, justice, piety and goodness.

The Prophet's 鑫 blessed proclamations include 'There is no obedience of the one who disobeys Allah,' and 'The creation is not to obey in the disobedience of the Creator'

When Abu Bakr Siddiq became Caliph he announced in his very first address:

'Obey me whilst I obey Allah and His Prophet 鑫, but if I disobey Allah and His Prophet 鑫 it is not incumbent upon you (to obey me).' (Kanz ul Ammaal)

Ameer ul Momineen Ali said in one of his sermons:

> 'It is incumbent upon you to obey me in whatever I order
> you from the obedience of Allah, whether you like it or not,
> and whatever I order you from the disobedience of Allah is
> not incumbent upon any one of you to obey. Obedience is
> only in the good, obedience is only in the good, obedience is
> only in the good.' (Kanz ul ammaal)

Ubaada bin Saamit narrates that the Prophet ﷺ said:

> 'Soon after me there will be Imams over you who will order
> you (things) you know nothing of and will do acts which are
> forbidden so it is not upon you to obey such Imams.' (As
> Siraaj ul Muneer)

Talha bin Ubayd narrates from the Prophet ﷺ:

> 'People! Be aware! Allah does not accept the prayer of the
> Imam who does not rule according to what Allah revealed.'
> (Al Mustadrak)

Imam Nawawi in the Shara of Sahih Muslim writes:

> 'There is the ijma of the Ulama upon the compulsion to obey
> in non sinful matters and upon the prohibition to obey in sin.
> Qaadhi Iyaad and others have narrated this Ijma.' (Nawawi
> ala'l Muslim)

Imam Nawawi also writes in another place:

> 'Qaadhi Iyaad has written 'Ijma of the ulama exists upon
> the principle that the Imamate of a kafir (disbeliever) does
> not become established, and if he becomes a kafir (during
> his Imamate) he will become relieved (of his imamate); and

similarly (there is Ijma) if he forsakes establishing the prayer or calling towards it, and similarly, the majority of the ulama believe, if he becomes embroiled in Bid'a.' (Nawawi ala'l Muslim)

In a third place Imam Nawawi writes:

'Qaadhi Iyad has stated that if he (the Imam) becomes a kaafir, or changes the shariah or undertakes bid'a he (automatically) comes out of the position of rule and following him becomes void. It becomes compulsory upon the Muslims to stand up to him and remove and replace him with a just Imam. This is only when such is possible for them. If not and only a small group stands up it is compulsory upon it to remove the kaafir. However it is only compulsory to remove the person of bid'a when that group believes it is able to do so. If it perceives its inability to do so then it is not compulsory upon them to stand against him and the Muslims should emigrate from that land for another to escape with their deen.' (Nawawi ala'l Muslim)

Imam Shafi'ee states :

'Verily the Imam is disqualified by fisq and kufr, and similarly so is every Qaadhi and Ameer. The basic principle is that a faasiq (transgressor) is not worthy of governing because if he does not care about himself (by committing fisq) how can he care for others?' (Shara Aqaaid)

Even if there is disagreement over whether a faasiq and faajir Imam automatically becomes disqualified there is unanimity that he is worthy of removal. Consequently Allaama Taftazaani writes:

'Similarly, as a result of this fisq, the Imam automatically becoming discharged is a point of disagreement, most believe that he does not automatically become discharged because of fisq and this is the preferred opinion of Imams Shafi'ee and Abu Haneefa. Both opinions are narrated from Imam Muhammad. However the worthiness of such a faasiq Imam to be removed is agreed upon, i.e. there is no disagreement in it' (Shara Aqaaid)

The statements of Allah, His Prophet 鸞, the Khulafa ur Raashideen, the Imams and the Ulama all confirm that a faasiq does not have the ability to become the ruler of the Muslims. His Imamate and rule is void and obeying and following him is unlawful.

Allaama Abdul Ghani Naabulisi writes 'Aafaani in *Shara Johara* states that there are five conditions for an Imam (of the Emirate): Islam, Balugh (of age); Intellect; Free and Pure of fisq in belief and actions. This is because a faasiq does not have the ability to command the matters of the deen, nor can his commands and prohibitions be trusted and the matters of deen and duniya will be destroyed under him so how can he be worthy of governorship and rule? Who would be able to counter his evil? Is the wolf shepherding the sheep not strange?!'

Consequently if a faassiq and oppressor does take over the Imamate or is appointed the Imam he will still remain a faasiq and oppressor and will not be deemed a just and rightful ruler solely because he has become the ruler! (he will be the *de facto* ruler but that no way means he is the *de jure* ruler)

The Imams have, in light of the Quran and Sunnah, mentioned some principles in standing up to such tyrant rulers:

If the faasiq and dhaalim (tyrant) restricts his fisq and dhulm (tyranny) to himself and it has no impact upon the people, e.g. he transgresses and fornicates in private but dispenses justice etc fairly then it is not permissible to revolt against such a ruler simply because of his personal or private transgressions as through him the matters of the State are being fulfilled properly. This is even despite him being a grave sinner and punishable near Allah for his personal fisq and fujoor.

The ahadith that teach us not to quarrel with a faasiq and faajir Ameer and Imam are about this kind of Imam whose fisq is confined to himself and is discrete. Ubaada bin Saamit narrates that he went to the Prophet 🌸 who said to him:

> 'O Ubaada, listen and obey in both ease and difficulty, in happiness and unhappiness, and give him priority over yourself, even if he takes your wealth and flogs you on your back, but do not do so if it is open rebellion against Allah.' (Kanz ul Ammaal)

This hadith clearly demonstrates that it is not permissible to obey a ruler whose fisq is clearly proven to be undertaken in the open. The imam whose fisq transcends himself and begins to affect the general public will, it is agreed upon, become worthy of removal, if not automatically invalid. If the muslims have the power it is compulsory upon them to remove and replace him with a just imam. If they do not have the power it is upon them to show patience and supplicate to Allah and for fear of fitna and wasting lives they should not rebel for they are 'ma'zoor' (excused) and there is danger of great loss.

We now need to consider if Yazeed had any evil traits. Undoubtedly not only was he a faasiq, faajir, drunkard and oppresser, but he undertook such shameful and wicked deeds and acts that some great scholars deemed him a kaafir (as will be mentioned later). As a result of these Imam Husayn did not deem him worthy of becoming the Imam of the Muslims and according to the rules of Shariah his caliphate had not been unanimously established. In addition Imam Husayn had never accepted his caliphate and deemed his rule invalid and it compulsory to remove him. However Imam Husayn was aware of recent history and the great bloodshed and discord within the Muslims and knew that all the Muslims would not stand up with him and so opted for patience and left Madeenah for the sanctity of Makkah, for Allah had promised *'Whoever entered it entered it in security'*.

However due to the relentless letters and delegations from Kufa and then Muslim bin Aqeel's eye witness testimony from there that things were sound Imam Husayn was assured that he had enough supporters to make a successful stand against Yazeed. It was after this assurance that he left Makka. Ibn Khuldun writes:

'And as for Imam Husayn, when Yazeed's fisq and fujoor became evident to all his contemporaries the Shia of Kufa wrote to Imam Husayn claiming that they would obey him and stand up (against Yazeed). Thus Imam Husayn thought it was incumbent to stand up to Yazeed in light of his fisq, especially if he had the means to do so. Imam Husayn believed that he had the right and worthiness and the power and means to do so. As for his right and worthiness he was undoubtedly correct, if anything he underestimated his right and worth. But as for his power and means (based on the promises of the people of Kufa) he was mistaken. May Allah have mercy upon him.' (Muqaddima Ibn Khuldun)

He adds further on:

'You have seen that Imam Husayn made a mistake (based on the false promises of support from the people of Kufa) but that was only in a worldly matter, which is not detrimental. As for the Shari (legal) matter he made no mistake as he believed (rightly) he was more worthy than him (Yazeed).' (Muqaddima Ibn Khuldun)

As for those companions who tried to stop Imam Husayn from standing up against Yazeed, it was not because they deemed it against the Shariah or tantamount to rebelling against a rightful Caliph, but merely because they knew the people of Kufa to be untrustworthy and not those who would fulfil their promise of allegiance and support. Thus according to these companions the causes for standing up (the physical ability to do so) against Yazeed did not exist and so tried to stop Imam Husayn from doing so. On the other hand the repeated requests from the people of Kufa, their swearing allegiance upon the hand of Muslim bin Aqeel and Muslim bin Aqeel's positive reports had convinced Imam Husayn that the need to stand up (based on the physical ability from the support of the people of Kufa) existed. Thus the only disagreement between Imam Husayn and the companions was over the existence of the need to stand up against Yazeed, and not whether such standing up was against the Shariah.

Unfortunately the people of Kufa, despite their claims of loving the Ahl ul Bait, proved right the fears of the companions and rendered the ultimate betrayal, leaving Imam Husayn unable to bring about a revolution against the Yazeedi rule. Instead, in front of his family and household, he, his children and faithful companions, had to taste the pure liquor of martyrdom in a very painful and torturous way. However this insignificant believes that Imam Husayn did lead a revolution, whose effects though not immediately apparent, are still being felt to this day and his martyrdom continues to serve as a shining example.

This proves that Imam Husayn's stand was not tantamount to needless rebellion or discord on the Earth but was to rid the 'Umma of an oppressive government and save it from the torture and oppression of Yazeed. Shah Abdul Aziz Dehlvi writes:

> 'Imam Husayn's stand (against Yazeed) (was not to establish the Rightful Caliphate as that had ended thirty years earlier, but rather) was based on saving the 'Umma from the tyranny of Yazeed. Helping the oppressed against the oppressor is one of the obligations of the deen.' (Fataawa Azeezi)

After this he explains 'As for the hadith in Mishkaat Shareef in which the Prophet ﷺ forbid rebelling and standing against a ruler, be he a tyrant, that is about the situation when that ruler takes full control of government without any opposition or dispute. However in this particular case the people of Makkah, Madeenah and Kufa had never accepted the filthy Yazeed's taking control of government, and great dignitaries such as Imam Husayn, Abdullah bin Abbas, Abdullah bin Zubair and Abdullah bin Umar etc had not taken Yazeed's Bai'a (pledged allegiance). Thus Imam Husayn's stand against him was to rid the 'Umma and not to set up his own rule (revolt (*rafa*) takes place after accepting the ruler whilst ridding (*dafa*) takes place before accepting the ruler), the stand against the ruler prohibited in hadith is the *rafa* (revolt) of a ruler and the difference between Rafa and Dafa is well known in the matters of Fiqh'. (Fataawa Azeezi)

Mulla Ali Qaari writes:

'The *afwaa* (rancour) of some of the ignorant that Imam Husayn was a rebel has been rejected by Ahl us Sunnah wa'l Jamaah. Maybe this (rancour) is the rubbish of the Kharijites who have strayed from the straight path.' (Shara Fiqh ul Akbar)

This statement of Mulla Ali Qaari, a leading Imam of the Ahl us Sunnah, clearly proves that those who call Imam Husayn a rebel and the filthy Yazeed a rightful Caliph cannot be from the Ahl us Sunnah, instead they are Kharijite and Yazeedites for calling Imam Husayn a rebel can only be their drivel!

In summary, it has been proven from authentic legal (Shari) sources that Imam Husayn did not deem Yazeed, who was a faasiq and faajir, worthy of the Imamate and rule of the Muslims. In addition his caliphate had not been established according to the rules of Shariah and nor did Imam Husayn ever pledge allegiance to him and so Yazeed's obedience was not incumbent upon him. Thus whatever Imam Husayn did against him was in accordance with the Quran and Sunnah. Consequently calling Imam Husayn a rebel and insurgent is absolutely wrong and the greatest form of ignorance and a slur on both Imam Husayn and the Ahl ul bait and clear proof of one's enmity and hatred of the Prophet's 🕌 Household.

YAZEED'S CHARACTER

Was Yazeed a knowledgeable, wise, pious, god fearing, prayer and fast establishing, extremely righteous, exceedingly kind and good natured man?

Or was he a faasiq, faajir, drunk and a tyrant? And is it permissible to perform 'la'na' (curse) upon him?

Yazeed was in no way a knowledgeable, wise, pious, god fearing, establisher of prayer and fasts and extremely righteous man. The fact of him being a faasiq, faajir and drunkard is undisputed. Where there is disagreement is over him being a kaafir and performing of 'la'na upon him. This will be explained below.

Allah Ta'aala had blessed His Prophet ﷺ with knowledge of *maa kaana wa maa yakun* 'what had happened and what was to happen'. The Prophet ﷺ presented before the companions all the events from the beginning of the creation to the entering of the people of Paradise into Paradise. As a result Ameer ul Momineen Syeduna Umar narrated:

> 'The Prophet ﷺ informed us of the beginning of the creation to the entering of the people of Jannah into their positions and the people of Hell into their positions. Whoever remembered remembered and whoever forgot forgot.' (Bukhaari)

Hudayfa narrates:

'The Prophet ﷺ stayed with us and did not leave anything that was to happen up until the establishing of Qiyaama, except informing us of it.' (Muslim)

He also narrates:

'The Prophet ﷺ did not leave out any leader of any sedition (*fitna*) that would occur to the end of the world. He said they will number more than 300 and told us of their names and their father's names and the names of their tribes.' (Mishkaat)

These narrations reveal that the Prophet ﷺ had revealed all that was to happen until Qiyaama and had identified the names of the founders of the fitnas that were to take place. As a result he had also foretold of the Yazeedi fitna. Abu Ubayda narrates that the Prophet ﷺ said:

'The rule of my umma will continue upon justice until a man (first) destroys it, he will be from the Banu Umayya called Yazeed.' (Al Bidaaya wan Nihaaya, As Sawaaiq ul Muharriqa)

Abu Darda narrates he heard the Prophet ﷺ saying:

'The one who will change my way will be a man from the Banu Umayya called Yazeed.' (As Sawwaiq ul Muharriqa)

Abu Zar narrates that he heard the Prophet ﷺ saying:

'The first one who will change my way will be a man from the Banu Umayya.' (Al Bidaaya wa Nihaaya)

Imam Bukhaari's Sahih has a whole chapter entitled 'The Chapter in the Prophet's ﷺ statement that his umma will be destroyed at the hands of foolish young men.' In this chapter the following prophetic statement narrated by Abu Hurayra is mentioned:

> 'My umma will be destroyed at the hands of some young men of the Quraysh. On hearing this Marwaan said 'May Allah's La'na be upon those young men.' Abu Hurayra responded 'If I wanted I could tell you their names.' (Bukhaari)

This hadith reveals that the umma will be destroyed at the hands of a few Qurayshi boys. This does not mean that they will be immature in years, rather they will be of age but will be immature in intelligence, understanding and foresight. In explaining the above hadith Imam Ibn Hajar Asqalaani writes:

> 'I state that the word child and young man with *tasgeer* (diminutive) is used for the one who is weak in intelligence, understanding and deen. Here such a person is meant even if he is mature (in age) because there was no Caliph from the Banu Umayya who was immature in terms of years'. (Fath ul Baari)

The noteworthy point from this Prophetic narration is that he foretold his Umma would be destroyed at the hands of naive young men. In other words their lack of intelligence and understanding will destroy not a few people but the whole umma and forever end its unity and understanding and divide it into pieces by creating differences that would persist until the end and be the cause of its destruction.

A question here is who were these young men of the Quraysh who became the cause of the Umma's destruction? Let us view the statements of the Prophet ﷺ and the leading scholars of this umma:

Shaykh Muhaqqiq Shah Abdul Haq Muhaddith Ad Dehlvi writes in explaining this hadith:

'It is in *Mujma Al Bahaar* that Abu Hurayra knew of these people by name and face but through fear of fisaad would never expose them. This (hadith) refers to Yazeed bin Ameer Muaawiya, Ibn Ziyaad and the other young men of Banu Umayya like them, may Allah disgrace them all. It was from them that the murder and imprisonment of the Ahl ul Bait took place, as did the killing of the good muhaajireen and ansaar. Furthermore the destruction of people's lives and property perpetrated by Hujjaaj, the Ameer of Abdul Malik bin Marwaan, and Suleman bin Abdul Malik and his offspring are before everyone.' (Isha t'ul Lumaat).

Abu Hurayra narrates the Prophet ﷺ saying:

'I seek Allah's refuge from the emirate of the children.' He was asked 'How will the emirate of the children be?' He replied 'If you obey them you will be destroyed (in the deen) and if you disobey them they will destroy you (in the world) by taking your life or your property, or even both.' (Fath ul Baari)

Abu Saeed narrates from the Prophet ﷺ:

'The degenerate will come after the year 60 Hijri and will lose the prayer and follow his desires and will soon be entered into the *Gayy* (a painful valley of Hell).' (Al Bidaaya wa Nihaaya)

Abu Hurayra narrates from the Prophet ﷺ:

'Seek Allah's refuge from the year 60 and from the emirate of the children.' (Al bidaaya wa nihaaya)

Abu Hurayra narrates that the Prophet ﷺ said:

'There is destruction for the Arabs from the evil that will commence in the year 60; trusts will be seen as booty, sadaqah as ransom, testimony for those they know, and rule based on personal desires.' (Kanz ul Ammaal)

These ahadith clearly show that that rule of these naive young men will begin in the year 60 and we know Yazeed took to the throne in the year 60. The rule of these brats will be such that following them will lead to the destruction of the deen whilst disobeying them will lead to the destruction of life and property. It was for this reason that the Prophet 🕌 said to Ka'b bin Ujza:

'O Ka'b bin Ujza! I place you in Allah's refuge from the rule of the fools'. Ka'b pleaded 'Yaa Rasoolallah, what is the rule of the fools?' He explained 'Soon there will be rulers who when they speak will lie and when they act will oppress. So whoever will come and validate their lies and aid them in their oppression will not be from me and I will not be from him and tomorrow (on qiyaamah) he will not come to my fountain (of kawthar). And whoever will not go to them and will not validate their lies and will not aid them in their oppression will be from me and I from him and tomorrow (on qiyaamah) he will come to my fountain.' (Kanz ul Ammaal)

This hadith highlights the signs of these foolish rulers; lies and oppression; and warns that whoever supports them and validates them is not from the Prophet 🕌 and will not be able to approach his fountain. So who are these foolish, lying and oppressive rulers at whose hands the Umma's deen and duniya will be destroyed?

Imam Ibn Hajar Asqalaani narrates from Ibn Abi Shayba:

'Even when walking in the marketplaces Abu Hurayra would plead 'O Allah do not allow me to witness the year 60 or the rule of the youth.' (Fath ul Baari)

Allaama Imam Ibn Hajar Haytami writes :

'Abu Hurayra had knowledge from the Prophet ﷺ of these matters mentioned in Yazeed. Thus he would supplicate 'O Allah, I seek your refuge from the beginning of the Year 60 and the rule of the youth.' So Allah accepted his plea and he died in the year 59, Ameer Muaawiya died in Year 60 and Yazeed took over. Abu Hurayra, from the Prophet's ﷺ information, was aware of Yazeed's rule from that year and his vile condition and so sought refuge from that year.' (As Sawaaiq ul Muharriqa)

Mulla Ali Qaari in explaining the 'rule of the youth' writes:

'It means the rule of ignorant youngsters like Yazeed bin Ameer Muaawiya; the offspring of Hakim bin Marwaan and their like. It is mentioned that in a dream the Prophet ﷺ saw them playing upon his pulpit.'

After mentioning this hadith Imam Hafiz Ibn Hajar Asqalaani writes:

'In it is a signal that the first of these youth will be in the Year 60. And it was like that for Yazeed became Caliph that year and remained so until the Year 64, when he died.' (Fath ul Baari)

In another place he writes:

'The first of them (foolish youth) was Yazeed, as proven by Abu Hurayra's statement regarding the start of the Year 60 and the emirate of the youth. Yazeed removed all the elder people from the governorships of most of the large cities and replaced them with his younger relatives.' (Fath ul Baari)

Allaama Badr ud Deen Aini and Allaama Kirwaani in explaining the Prophet's 🕌 statement 'My umma will be destroyed at the hands of foolish young men' write:

> 'The first of them was Yazeed, who should get what he deserves, he mostly removed the elder statesmen from the governorships of the large cities and replaced them with young men from his relatives.' (Umda tul Qaari; Haashiya Bukhari)

In explaining the same hadith Mulla Ali Qaari writes:

> 'The statement *at the hands of the young men*' means the hands of those youth who had not yet reached the perfection of intellect and those who paid no regard to the honourable companions. It is clear that they are those who killed Uthman and fought against Ali and Husayn. Muzhir said that it refers to those who came after the Khulafa ur Rashideen such as Yazeed and Abd al Malik bin Marwan etc.' (Mirqaat)

In a second work Imam Mulla Ali Qaari writes:

> 'It refers to Yazeed bin Ameer Muaawiya for he sent Muslim bin Uqba to the Peaceful Madeenah and gave him freedom for three days and many great people of Madeenah were killed.' (Shara Shifa)

In explaining this hadith Allaama Ali bin Ahmad wrote:

> 'Of them is Yazeed bin Muaawiya and the like from the rulers of the Banu Umayya. Verily it was them who killed the Ahl ul Bait and the great Muhaajireen. The meaning of the hadith 'people will be destroyed' means because of their longing and desire of government and killings.' (Siraaj un Muneer Shara Jaame Muneer)

31

Imran bin Hussain narrates:

'The Prophet ﷺ died disliking three tribes; Thaqeef; Banu Haneefa and Banu Umayya.' (Tirmidhi, Mishkaat)

In explaining this hadith Shaykh Shah Abdal Haque Muhaddith Ad Dehlvi explains:

'The tyrant Hujjaaj bin Yusuf, who imprisoned and killed 120,000 muslims, was from the Thaqeef tribe. The imposter Musaylma, who claimed to be a prophet, was from the Banu Haneefa tribe whilst oppressors such as Yazeed and Ibn Ziyaad who killed Imam Husayn were from the Banu Umayya tribe. Whatever Ibn Ziyaad did he did on the command and with the consent of Yazeed and it was not just Yazeed and Ibn Ziyaad, for others of the Banu Umayya were no less in their dark acts. Furthermore it has been mentioned in the ahadith that in a dream the Prophet ﷺ saw monkeys playing and jumping upon his pulpit and explained it as the Banu Umayya. Apart from these there are many other matters, but what can one say?!' (Isha'tul Lumaat)

Hudayfa narrates:

'I asked 'Yaa Rasoolallah, will there be evil after this goodness (that we now have)?' He replied 'Yes' I asked 'What will be the salvation (from it)?' He explained 'The sword (i.e. fighting).' I asked 'And will there be any (bad) left after the sword?' He said 'Yes, it will be the government established in the wrong way with people not accepting it with their hearts and it being forced upon them' I asked 'What will happen then?' He revealed 'People will call towards misguidance. If at that time you have a Caliph obey him, even if he whips you on your back and takes your wealth, obey him, if not go and die in a hole under a tree.' (Mishkaat)

Below this hadith Shah Walliullah Muhaddith Ad Dehlvi writes 'The ones calling towards misguidance were Yazeed in Shaam, Mukhtaar in Iraq and their like.' (Hujja t'ul Bulaaga)

The Prophet's ﷺ statements; Abu Hurayra's statement (which holds the rank of Marfooh) and the statements of the commentators of ahahdith inform us that the first of these Sunnah distorting, foolish, naive, deceitful, callers to misguidance young men was Yazeed, with whom the destruction of the Umma began! The dark events of his four year rule can be summarised as follows:

In Year 61 the tragedy of Karbala took place in which the Household of the Prophet ﷺ, the darling son of the final Prophet's ﷺ darling daughter and the lady of paradise; the coolness of the emperor of Wilaaya; the chief of the youth of Paradise Imam Husayn and his sons, nephews, brothers and friends were, in broad daylight, mercilessly and callously murdered in a state of thirst and hunger in a foreign land before the gaze of their women and children. Not only that but their blessed bodies were trampled by horses, their tents looted and burned and the veils ripped off from their women. After that the daughters of the Prophet ﷺ were put onto camels and paraded through the streets and alleyways before being presented in the court of Yazeed before the gaze of strange men. In this way the Prophet's ﷺ family was brutally humiliated.

In the year 63 the tragedy of Hurra took place in which 700 of the Prophet's ﷺ companions and their children whilst another 10,000 young and old ordinary inhabitants of Madeenah were mercilessly and bloodily murdered. After being given the freedom of the city for three days Yazeed's army entered the houses and raped the pure and innocent women of the Prophet's ﷺ neighbourhood.

In the year 64 Yazeed's army attacked Makka and the sanctity of the Ka'ba was severely violated. With a catapult the Ka'ba was struck by artillery and its walls were shaken and it's cloth burnt. Alongwith this the haraam was made halal.

As a result of these oppressive and shameful acts – which shook the whole umma - some of the great scholars of the umma declared

Yazeed a Kaafir and deemed it permissible to curse him (send La'na upon him). Imam Ahmad bin Hanbal's son Saalih narrates 'I asked my father whether one should take Yazeed as a friend or curse him. Imam Ahmad responded:

> 'O Son, can there ever be anyone who believes in Allah and (still) has Yazeed as a friend? And why should I not curse the one whom Allah has cursed in His book'; I asked 'Where has Allah cursed Yazeed in His book?' He explained 'In the verse *'May it not be [the case] with you that if you were to turn away, you would then cause sedition in the land and sever your kinship ties?' (Quran 47:22)* O son, could there be any greater sedition than this murder (of Husayn)?' (As Sawaaiq ul Muharriqa)

Anas narrates that the Prophet ﷺ said:

> 'Whoever harmed a Muslim verily harmed me and whoever harmed me verily harmed Allah.' (Siraaj ul Muneer Shara Jaame us Sageer)

Ameer ul Momineen Ali narrates from the Prophet ﷺ:

> 'Whoever hurt a hair of mine verily hurt me and whoever hurt me verily hurt Allah.' The narration of Abu Nuaim has additionally 'So may Allah's curse be upon him.' (Siraaj ul Muneer Shara Jaame us Sageer)

Abu Hurayra narrates that Abu Lahab's daughter Sabee'a came to the Prophet ﷺ and pleaded:

> 'Yaa Rasoolallah people say that I am the daughter of the fuel of the Hellfire.' On hearing this the Prophet ﷺ stood up in great anger and said 'What do people think they are doing hurting me about my relatives?! Remember whoever hurt me in reality hurt Allah!' (Zarqaani ala'l Muwaahib)

Look carefully at this, Abu Lahab is undoubtedly the fuel of the Hellfire. The Quran states *{'He will soon enter a Fire, full of flames}* (111:3)' But when people taunted his daughter about it it hurt the Prophet ﷺ and hurting the Prophet ﷺ is a cause of hurting Allah, even though what they were saying was true. They should not have said it in a way that hurt the relatives of the Prophet ﷺ and caused hurt to Allah and His Prophet ﷺ. From this one can try to sense how much pain those who killed the Prophet's ﷺ beloved grandson would have caused Allah and His Prophet ﷺ.

The purpose of all these ahadith is to teach the honour and respect of the Prophet's ﷺ household and to warn against hurting and harming them because if hurting an ordinary Muslim, or the Prophet's ﷺ hair, or his relatives, in effect hurts the Prophet ﷺ and Allah then without a doubt hurting his offspring, who are a part of his body, hurts the Prophet ﷺ. And the Quran clearly curses those who hurt Allah and His Prophet ﷺ *"Indeed those who hurt Allah and His Messenger, Allah has cursed them in this world and the Hereafter, and has prepared for them a humiliating punishment." (Quran33:57)'*

Abdullah bin Abbas stated:

'This verse was revealed when Abdullah bin Ubayy and his companions slandered Syeda Aisha. The Prophet ﷺ then delivered a sermon and said 'Who will help me against the man who has hurt me (by slandering my wife)' (Durr e Mukhtaar)

Thus whoever hurt the Prophet's ﷺ honourable wife hurt Allah and His Prophet and is worthy of La'na. Yazeed and his aides hurt and humiliated the Prophet's ﷺ family in a heinous manner that makes the soul tremble by just thinking about it, so they are without doubt worthy of La'na.

Sa'd bin Abi Waqaas states that the Prophet 🌸 said:

> 'Whoever intends bad for the people of Madeenah will be dissolved by Allah like salt is dissolved in water.' (Sahih Muslim)

The words of another narration are:

> 'No one intends evil for the people of Madeenah except Allah will dissolve him in the fire of hell like tin' (Muslim)

Jaabir narrates that the Prophet 🌸 said:

> 'Whoever frightens the people of Madeenah Allah will frighten him on the day of Qiyaama.' In another narration it is additionally 'And Allah's La'na and wrath is upon him.' (Sahih Ibn Hibbaan; Siraaj ul Muneer)

Ubaada bin Saamit narrates the Prophet's 🌸 statement:

> 'Whoever frightens the people of Madeenah through oppression will be frightened by Allah on the day of Qiyaama and upon him is the La'na of Allah, the Angels and all the people. On the day of Qiyaama Allah will not accept his obligatory or supergotary prayers.' (Wafa ul Wafaa; Jazb ul Quloob)

Abdullah bin Umar narrates from the Prophet 🌸:

> 'Whoever hurts the people of Madeenah Allah will hurt him and upon him is the La'na of Allah, the Angels and all the people. On the day of Qiyaama Allah will not accept his obligatory or voluntary (acts).' (Siraaj ul Muneer)

These ahadith prove that whoever hurts, frightens or even intends bad towards the people of Madeenah will be dissolved in Hell by Allah and the La'na of Allah, the Angels and all the people will be upon him. Indeed none of his prayers or deeds will be accepted. We have previously described how Yazeed had Madeenah attacked and subjected to acts of oppression and torture that leave humanity in a state of shame. In light of these ahadith Yazeed and his aides are worthy of La'na.

Mulla Ali Qaari quotes the statement of Imam Ibn Himaam:

'There is disagreement over the Kufr of Yazeed. Those who say he is do so based on the matters narrated about him which prove his kufr, such as making wine permissible and saying that by killing Imam Husayn and his companions he had exacted revenge for the killing of his ancestors and chiefs at Badr and other similar narrations. Perhaps it was because of these that Imam Ahmad bin Hanbal denoted him Kaafir as he had evidence of his such statements.' (Shara Fiqh ul Akbar)

Allaama Saad ud Deen Taftazaani, author of Shara ul Aqaaid, writes:

'The truth is that Yazeed approved the killing of Imam Husayn and was happy with it and the humiliation of the Prophet's ﷺ household. These are matters that are narrated with tawaatur, even though in narration they may each be singular. Consequently we do not remain silent about him regarding his imaan (we say) may Allah's La'na be upon him and his helpers and supporters.' (Shara ul Aqaaid)

The author of Nabraas, the commentator of Shara ul Aqaaid writes:

'Of those who cursed (performed Lana upon) Yazeed is the Muhaddith Ibn Jowzi who wrote a book on this matter entitled 'Ar Radd al Muta'asib al Gabeed al Ma'ni an Dham il Yazeed'. Also amongst them (who cursed Yazeed) are Imam Ahmad bin Hanbal and Qaadhi Abu'l Ya'laa.' (Nabraas ala Shara ul Aqaaid).

These are the Ahl us Sunnah's renowned books of Aqeeda upon which the creed of the Ahl us Sunnah is based.

Imam Ibn Hajar Makki, the foundation of the Shafi'ee madhab, whom Mulla Ali Qaari described with the words 'Our Shaykh, al Aalim, Allaama, Ocean of understanding, Shaykh ul Islam, Mufti ul Anaam, Author of numerous books and famous writings, Molaaana, Sayyiduna, Sanaduna As Shaykh Shuaab ud Deen bin Hajar Al Makki, writes:

'Know that the Ahl us Sunnah disagree in the Takfeer (apostasy) of Yazeed bin Muaawiya and him being the heir to Ameer Muaawiya. A group claims that he is Kaafir. The statement of the grandson of Ibn Jowzi is well known (that) when the blessed head of Imam Husayn was brought to Damascus Yazeed gathered the people of Shaam and played with it with the stick he had in his hand and proclaimed the verses of Zubaree; 'If only my ancestors (killed at) Badr could witness this' and he also added two other verses which were clear Kufr. Ibn Jowzi added that it was not so strange that Ibn Ziyaad killed Imam Husayn, what was strange was Yazeed's disappointment and his striking Imam Husayn's teeth with his stick and imprisoning the family of the Prophet ﷺ and putting them upon the saddles of the camels. Ibn Jowzi mentioned many other such vile matters which are infamous about Yazeed. Furthermore Yazeed only sent the blessed head to Madeenah when it had begun to decay and his purpose behind this could have been nothing except the humiliation and the degradation of the blessed head. This is despite the fact that the funeral and shrouding of even the corpses of the Kharijites and rebels is permitted (so the rank of the son of the Prophet ﷺ should be higher!). Had Yazeed not had the malice and hatred of jahilliya or the thirst for revenge of Badr he would have shown respect to the head of Imam Husayn after its arrival and shrouded and buried it and treated the family of the Prophet ﷺ in the best way.' (As Sawaaiq Al Muharriqa)

Allaama Shaykh Muhammad bin Ali Isbaan writes:

'Verily Imam Ahmad has mentioned his kufr, and undoubtedly his knowledge and prudence would not have allowed him to do so until matters about Yazeed's kufr had become clearly proven to him. So undoubtedly these matters which necessitate kufr must have been undertaken by Yazeed. Furthermore, a group of ulama did agree with his Takfeer (deeming Kaafir) such as Ibn Jowzi and others. As for Yazeed being a faasiq, there is undoubtedly the Ijma of the Ulama upon this, many ulama have even deemed it permissible to perform La'na upon Yazeed by specifically mentioning his name, this is also narrated about Imam Ahmad. Ibn Jowzee said that Imam Qadhi Abu Ya'la had written a whole book on those worthy of La'na and had mentioned Yazeed in it.' (As'aaf ur Raagibeen)

The Qutb ul Aqtaab, Ghoth ul Thaqalaain, Shaykh ul Shuyookh ul Aalam, Imam ul Asfiya, Muhayy ud deen Abu Muhammad Syed Abdul Qadir Al Jilaani, Al Hasani, Al Husayni writes 'And of the virtues of Ashura; verily Imam Husayn was martyred on the day of Ashura. Umm e Salama narrates:

'The Prophet ﷺ was at my house when Syeduna Husayn came to him and I stood looking at them from the door. I saw Syeduna Husayn playing on the Prophet's ﷺ chest whilst the Prophet ﷺ held some dust in his hand and tears flowed from his eyes. After Imam Husayn had left I approached the Prophet ﷺ and pleaded 'May my parents be forsaken over you, I saw dust in your hands and tears in your eyes'. He explained 'Whilst Husayn was playing upon my chest and I was enjoying it Jibril came to me and handed me the dust upon which Husayn would be killed. That is why I cried.'

Furthermore Hasan Basri narrates that Sulayman bin Abd ul Malik saw the Prophet ﷺ in a dream and was given glad tidings and endowed with kindness and favours. When morning broke he relayed the dream to Hasan Basri who explained 'Maybe you have performed an act of kindness to the Ahl ul Bait?' He replied 'Yes I have; I found the head of Imam Husayn in Yazeed's lockers and wrapped it in 5 silken sheets and I and my companions prayed (the funeral) upon it and buried it'. Hasan Basri explained 'Surely it is because of this act that the Prophet ﷺ is pleased with you and has been kind with you and given you glad tidings.' Suleman bin Abdul Malik favoured Hassan Basri and presented him with lots of gifts and rewards.

Hamza bin Zayyaat narrates 'I saw the Prophet ﷺ and Syeduna Ibraheem, the Khalilullah, in a dream. They were both praying the funeral over the grave of Imam Husayn.

Also Abu Nasr told us from his father from Usama who said that Imam Jafar Saadiq bin Imam Muhammad Baaqir revealed that on the day Imam Husayn was martyred 70,000 angels descended upon his grave and will cry until Qiyaama.' (Guniya t'ul Taalibeen; Baab Fadaail Aashura)

After this he writes:

'Verily Allah chose the most honoured, most greatest and most elevated of all days for the martyrdom of His Prophet's

🖼 son in order to raise his (Imam Husayn's) status and increase his virtue so that he could attain the rank of the martyred Khulafa ur Raashideen. Had it been permissible to make the day of Imam Husayn's martyrdom a day of grief (museeba) then the day of Monday was more worthy of being a day of grief for on that day Allah gave death to the Prophet 🖼.' (Guniya t'ul Taalibeen)

Shaykh al Muhaqqiq Allaama Shah Abd ul Haque Ad Dehlvi writes:

'Some of the ulama have exercised restraint with regards (La'na upon) the wretched Yazeed. There are some others however who have exaggerated and become so lost in the friendship of Yazeed that they claim he was the unanimous Ameer of the Muslims and his obedience was incumbent upon Imam Husayn. We seek Allah's protection from such a statement and such a belief. How can Yazeed become Ameer in the presence of Imam Husayn and when did all the Muslims ever agree upon him?!' All of the companions and Ta'bieen of his time rejected him and were outside his domain of obedience. A delegation from Madeenah was unwillingly forced to travel to Syria and Yazeed favoured them with grand hospitality and showered them with great gifts but when they witnessed his evil actions and reflected upon their dangerous outcomes they broke the bai'a on returning to Madeenah and announced that Yazeed was the enemy of Allah; a drunkard; waster of prayers, fornicator, faasiq and one who deemed the haram halal.

Some claim that Yazeed never ordered the murder of Imam Husayn and nor did he agree with it and did not rejoice on learning of his and his companions murders. These statements are also rejected and offensive, because this wretch's enmity of the Prophet's 🖼 household, and his joy over their killing and humiliation has reached the rank of tawaatur in terms of meaning, and rejecting it is a Takalluf and Mukaabira, tantamount to a baseless dispute.

Some state that the killing of Imam Husayn was (merely) a *kabeera* (Major sin) because killing an innocent Muslim is an act of sin and not an act of kufr (infidelity) and la'na is specifically for disbelievers. It is sad that those who make up such things do not recall the unambiguous hadith of the Prophet 🕊 that enmity with Syeda Fatima and her children, hurting and humiliating them, is in fact enmity with the Prophet 🕊, hurting him and dishonouring him and this undoubtedly results in kufr, la'na and residence in Hell. Allah undoubtedly states in the Quran *'Those who hurt Allah and His Prophet ... (33:57).'*

Some state that we do not know the state he died in for he may have repented from kufr and sinful acts and so died in the state of repentance. Imam Muhammad Gazaali in *Ihya ul Uloom* leans towards this view. (However) other ulama of the Salaf and elders of the Umma such as Imam Ahmad Ibn Hanbal and similar, for example Ibn Jowzee, who was very strict in defending the Sunna and Shariah, has in his book quoted the Salaf us Saliheen's La'na upon Yazeed. Others have prevented performing La'na whilst others have adopted restraint.

In conclusion, for us, Yazeed is the most detested. This wretch did to the umma what no one else did! (e.g.) after the murder of Imam Husayn and humiliation of the Ahl ul Bait he sent an army to sack Madeenah and ordered the killing of the Sahaaba and Ta'bieen. After that he ordered the conquering of Makka and he died during this. Thus in this state only Allah knows how he could have repented! May Allah protect our and the Muslim's hearts from the love and companionship of Yazeed and his helpers and everyone else who did or hoped for evil with the Household of the Prophet 🕊 and usurped their rights and did not follow the true path of their love and devotion. May Allah save us from their friendship and keep us in His protection. May Allah, through His favour and kindness, raise us and our friends as true devotees of the Prophet's 🌼 household and in Akhirah and this world keep us upon the Deen of Islam and their (the Ahl ul Bait's) path. Aameen, *Wa Huwa Qareeb ul Mujeeb*.' (Takmeel ul Imaan)

Imam Ahmad Qustalaani writes:

'Some of the ulama have performed La'na upon Yazeed, for example Allaama Saad udDeen Taftazaani's La'na upon Yazeed is narrated. This is because when he ordered the killing of Imam Husayn he became kaafir, and the majority of the ulama agree that it is permissible to send La'na upon the one who killed Imam Husayn; the one who ordered it; the one who allowed it and the one who agreed with it. The truth is that Yazeed's agreement with Imam Husayn's killing, his joy over it and his humiliating the Ahl ul Bait, is proven in meaning with tawaatur, even if it is made up of individual narrations. Thus we do not show restraint about him, rather about his Iman (we say) may Allah's La'na be upon him and on his helpers and supporters.' (Irshaad us Saari)

Allaama Jalaal ud Deen Suyooti writes:

'Allah's La'na be upon Imam Husayn's murderer Ibn Ziyaad and upon Yazeed too. Imam Husayn was killed at Karbala and it is a long story which the heart is not strong enough to bear. *Inna Lillahi wa Inna lillahi Raajioon*.' (Taareekh ul Khulafaa)

Ibn Taymiya writes:

'If someone calls Yazeed 'Imam son of Imam' and by that he only means that the Caliphate transferred to him like it did for all the Banu Umayya and Banu Abbas Caliphs then it is correct but it in no way implies that he is praiseworthy, respected or revered because not everyone who becomes a Caliph is from the Khulafa ur Raashideen or rightly guided imams. Simply becoming the ruler of people does not make one praiseworthy or rewardful, one is only worthy of praise and reward if one establishes justice, truth, honesty, orders the good, forbids the evil, and establishes Jihad and the boundaries imposed by Allah. Similarly through oppression, deceit, ordering evil, preventing good, disregarding the limits set by Allah, losing the rights of people and forsaking jihad, one is worthy of condemnation and reproach. Thus when Imam Ahmad ibn Hanbal was asked whether ahadith could be narrated from Yazeed he replied 'No! He is not worthy, Is he not the one who did what he did to the People of Hurra?! And when his son said that some people take Yazeed as a beloved he replied 'Can anyone with a shred of goodness like Yazeed?! His son then asked why he did not send La'na upon Yazeed and he replied 'Have you ever seen your father perform La'na upon anyone ?!' (Yazeed bin Ameer Muaawiya p29; Ibn Taymiyya Academy, Karachi)

These final words of Imam Ahmad bin Hanbal do not mean that he did not believe that Yazeed was worthy of La'na for you have read previously that Imam Ahmad ibn Hanbal proved the La'an upon Yazeed from the Quran.

Allaama Haafiz Ibn Katheer writes:

'Verily it is narrated that Yazeed was infamous for instruments of folly and play, drinking wine, singing, hunting, keeping good looking boys, playing music, keeping dogs and organising bear and monkey fights. There was never a day when he was not drunk. He used to race horses by riding monkeys upon them wearing golden hats. He would do the same with the boys when he raced them upon horses. Whenever any of the monkeys died he would be sad. It is said that the cause of his death was that he picked up one of these monkeys and was playing with it when it bit him. The historians have mentioned other despicable acts about him. Allah knows best.' (Al Bidaaya wa Nihaaya)

The Imam and great jurist of the Shafi'ee school Imam Al Kiyaalraasi was asked if Yazeed was from the Prophet's ﷺ companions and was it permissible to perform La'na upon him. He replied

'He was not from the companions because he was born during the time of Uthman. As for La'na there are two statements narrated from the likes of the Salaf; Imam Abu Haneefa, Imam Malik and Imam Ahmad bin Hanbal. *Tasreeh* (to perform La'na upon Yazeed by name) and *Talveeh* (to perform La'na in an unspecific but implying way such as 'La'na upon the Imam's killers'). However for us there is only one statement and that is *Tasreeh*. And why should it be otherwise for Yazeed hunted leopards, played chess and was always drinking wine. In one of his poems about wine he wrote:

> *'I say to my companions gathered by the drink and glass;*
> *to whom the heat of love is singing out;*
> *to take their portion of pleasure and joy;*
> *for every human will inevitably end, no matter how long (his life is).'*

The Faqhee Al Hiraasi wrote a very long discourse which we have not mentioned (for it is too long) in which he wrote that he turned the page over and wrote that had he more paper and allowed his pen to run free he could have described even more evils of this man (Yazeed).' (Hayaat ul Haiwaan)

Imam Mulla Ali Qaari writes about performing La'na upon Ameer Muaawiya:

'That is wholly impermissible. It is different to Yazeed, Ibn

Ziyaad et al for some of the ulama have deemed it permissible to perform La'na upon them, and furthermore Imam Ahmad ibn Hanbal was convinced of the kufr of Yazeed. However most of the ulama of the Ahl us Sunnah do not believe it permissible to perform La'na upon Yazeed because his kufr had not been clearly proven to them.' (Shara Shifaa)

Imam Rabbaani Mujaddid Alf Thaani wrote:

'Yazeed the wretch was not from the companions, no one disputes his wretchedness, no foreign kaafir would have dared do what that wretch did. Some of the ulama of the Ahl us Sunnah who refrain from performing La'na upon him do so not because they agree with him but because of the possibility of his repentance and retraction.' (Maktoobaat Shareef)

In another place he states:

'The wretch Yazeed is from amongst the Faasiqeen. Refraining from performing La'na upon him is based on an established principle of the Ahl us Sunnah which deems it impermissible to even perform La'na upon a specific Kaafir, except when it can be determined that he died in a state of Kufr, such as Abu Lahab and his wife. And (refraining from La'na) is definitely not because he (Yazeed) is not worthy of La'na for verily those who hurt Allah and His Prophet ﷺ have Allah's La'na upon them in this and the next world.' (Maktoobaat)

Molaana Abd al Hayy Lakhnavi writes;

'Some people through exaggeration and love for Yazeed claim that he became Caliph with the unanimous support of the Muslims and thus it was compulsory upon Imam Husayn to follow him. Do these people not ponder how he could be Ameer in the presence of Imam Husayn and when were the Muslims unanimous over his rule? A whole group of companions and their offspring never accepted or followed him, and there were some who did accept him but after witnessing his drunkardness, missing prayers, fornication and deeming permissible the impermissible broke their allegiance (bai'a) upon returning to Madeenah.

There are some who state that he never ordered the killing of Imam Husayn, nor did he agree with it and nor did he rejoice after the murders. This statement is also false, Allaama Taftazaani is Shara Aqaaid states 'The truth is that Yazeed approved the killing of Imam Husayn and was happy with it and the humiliation of the Prophet's ﷺ household. These are matters that are narrated with tawaatur, even though in narration they may each be singular. Consequently we do not remain silent about him regarding his imaan (we say) may Allah's La'na be upon him and his helpers and supporters.'

Some state that Imam Husayn's murder was a great sin but not an act of Kufr and La'na is specific only to the Kuffaar (disbelievers). The intellect of these people is sorrowful, do they not know that Kufr is one thing and giving pain to the Prophet ﷺ is another and has its own consequences for Allah said *'Indeed those who hurt Allah and His Messenger, Allah has cursed them in this world and the Hereafter, and has prepared for them a humiliating punishment.' (Quran33:57)*. Some state that no one knows his condition at the time of his death for he could have repented after undertaking his kufr and sin and may well have died in a state of repentance. Imam Gazaali in Ihya ul Uloom leans towards this but remember that the possibility of repentance is only a possibility, because the things that wretch did to this umma have probably not been done by anyone else! After the murder of Imam Husayn the humiliation of the Ahl ul Bait and his sending an army to sack Madeenah and kill its inhabitants. Furthermore during this 'Hurra' episode no Adhaan or prayer took place in the Prophet's 🕌 masjid for three days. After this that army attacked Makka, during which Abdullah bin Zubayr was killed in the very Haram. Yazeed died – and the world became pure – whilst he was busy in these kind of activities. His son Ameer Muaawiya (the junior) revealed his bad deeds upon the pulpit and only Allah knows well his hidden matters. There are some who deem it permissible to openly send La'na upon this wretch, from the Salaf and the Ulama of this umma (who do this) are Imam Ahmad ibn Hanbal and similar elders who have performed La'na upon him. Ibn Jowzi, who was very strict in protecting the Sunnah and Shariah, quotes the Salaf's La'na upon Yazeed in his book whilst Imam Taftazaani has performed La'na upon Yazeed and his helpers with great passion, whilst others have shown restraint and adopted silence. The path of safety is to neither remember that wretch with forgiveness and mercy but nor sully one's tongue with La'na which amongst the general public is specific for the disbelievers, such as for the damned Iblis, so even though his kufr is narrated there is no danger in restraining the tongue.' (Majmua tul Fataawa)

Shah Abdul Aziz Muhaddith Ad Dehlvi writes :

'Thus Imam Husayn refused to take the bai'a of Yazeed because he was a faasiq, drunkard and tyrant. Because of this Imam Husayn left for Makka.' (Sirr us Shahaadatain)

This same Shah Abdul Aziz Muhaddith Ad Dehlvi writes in response to a question in a fatwa:

Question: Restraint in performing La'na upon Yazeed is narrated about some people. What is the informed position?

Answer: About performing La'na upon Yazeed; restraint is based on the fact that there are differing accounts of the filthy Yazeed and the martyrdom of Imam Husayn. The understanding derived from some narrations is that Yazeed was in agreement with the killing of Imam Husayn and rejoiced over it and humiliated the Ahl ul bait and the family of the Prophet 饕. So for those ulama for whom these narrations are proven they have performed La'na upon Yazeed, thus Imam Ahmad bin Hanbal, KiyaaHaraasi from the Shafi'ee Fuqaha, and many other scholars have performed La'na upon Yazeed. Some narrations insist that Yazeed was saddened by the martyrdom of Imam Husayn and reproached Ibn Ziyaad and his helpers for it. In addition Yazeed was also ashamed that his deputy had carried out such an act. So for those ulama for whom this narration is proven they have prevented La'na upon Yazeed. Thus Imam Gazaali and some of the Shafi'ee ulama and most of the Hanafee ulama have forbidden La'na upon Yazeed. For some ulama both these narrations are proven and contradict one another and they cannot find a scholastic reason to prioritise one over the other, and so have remained silent on this matter out of caution. Whenever there are contradictory narrations and no reason can be found to give priority to one over the other it is compulsory upon the ulama to remain silent in ruling on the matter. This is the statement of Imam Abu Haneefa. However La'na upon Shimar and Ibn Ziyaad is unequivocally permissible for it is clearly proven that they were in agreement with the killing of Imam Husayn and were happy with it and there is no contradiction to this found in the narrations. Consequently none from the ulama have refrained from performing La'na upon Shimar and Ibn Ziyaad, indeed they are all in agreement in the permissibility of La'na upon Shimar and the ill-natured Ibn Ziyaad.' (Fataawa Azeezi Urdu)

In another place he also writes:

'Love of the Ahl ul Bait is from the obligations of Imaan (faith). It is a requirement of the Sunnah and love of the Ahl ul Bait to call Marwaan, upon whom be La'na, bad and the heart should be void of him. In specific he mistreated Imam Husayn and the Ahl ul bait. He had complete hatred for them, because of this we must stay totally aloof of this devil.' (Fataawa Azeezi)

Hazrat Bu Shah Qalandar Paani Patti writes in a couplet in his Mathnavi:

'For the sake of his duniya the ignorant
wicked Yazeed destroyed his deen;
When he married this fraudulent witch duniya he made lawful
the Syed's(Husayn) blood.'

Syed Shuaab ud deen Mahmud Aloosi, the Mufti of Baghdad, writes about the filthy Yazeed:

'I say what is prevalent in my mind, this *khabeeth* (scum) is not someone who confirms the messengership of the Prophet ﷺ. Without a doubt his collective actions against the inhabitants of the holy sanctities of Allah and His Prophet ﷺ, and his dealings with the Prophet's ﷺ offspring, both during and after their lifetimes, prove the absence of his confirmation of the Prophet's ﷺ messengership more than (the infidelity of) the one who throws pages of the Quran into filth. I do not believe that his condition was hidden from the great muslims of his time, however they were overwhelmed and oppressed and had no choice but to be patient and allow Allah's decree to take place. If we were to accept that this scum was a Muslim then he had amassed so many grave sins that they are beyond mention. For me it is correct and permissible to perform la'na on a specific person like Yazeed, even if we struggle to imagine a faasiq like him. It is apparent that he did not repent, and the possibility of his repentance is lesser than the possibility of his Iman! With Yazeed we will also include and refer to Ibn Ziyaad, Ibn Saad and his group. Thus may Allah's La'na be upon all of them and upon their helpers and supporters and their group and whoever leans towards them until Qiyaamah and until the time an eye still cries for *'Abu Abdullah'* Husayn.' (Tafseer Ruh ul Biyaan)

This very Muhaqqiq, Mudaqqiq and Mufassir Allaama Alossi Baghdaadi writes in another place:

'It is mentioned in a Sahih hadith that love for Imam Ali is a sign of Iman and hatred for him is a sign of hypocrisy. Consequently Umm e Salama narrated that the Prophet 🌸 once said to Imam Ali 'O Ali, no one loves you except a believer and no one hates you except a hypocrite.' (Nasai)

Furthermore, Zar bin Jaish narrates that Imam Ali himself said;

'By Allah Who created the tree from a seed, and revealed the human, the Prophet 🌸 made a promise to me that no one will love me except a believer and no one will hate me except a hypocrite.' (Ahmad, Tirmidhi, Nisai, Muslim)

After that Allaama Aloosi states;

'O Reader, what do you say about Yazeed, did he have love for Imam Ali or hatred? I do not believe you will doubt that he (Yazeed), upon whom be La'na, had the greatest hatred and enmity for Imam Ali and his two sons Hassan and Husayn, which is proven from the Tawaatur ahahdih. Thus you have no choice but to say that he is a La'een (damned) hypocrite.' (Ruh ul Ma'aani)

Allaama Qaadhi Thanaa ullah Paani Patti writes;

'Yazeed and his friends rejected (performed kufr) the blessings Allah had bestowed upon them and rose up in enmity of the Prophet's 🕌 family and unjustifiably martyred Imam Husayn. Yazeed also undertook Kufr with the deen of Muhammad, to the extent that he recited the following verses at the time of Imam Husayn's murder; 'Where are my ancestors to witness my revenge against the family of Muhammad and the Banu Hashim?!' and at the end proclaimed 'I would not have been from Jundub had I not taken revenge from the children of Ahmad for what they did'. In addition he permitted wine and about it wrote 'The treasure of wine is in a vessel like silver, and the stick is full of grapes and is like the stars, the density of this bushel of grapes is like the turret of the sun, the east of this sun (wine) is the hand of the inn keeper and its west is my mouth. If wine was made haram in the deen of Ahmad then drink it upon the deen of Maseeh ibn Maryam (i.e. deem it halal).' (Tafseer Mazhari)

He also writes in his Maktoobaat;

'In summary Yazeed's kufr is proven from trustworthy narrations, he is worthy of La'na. Even though there is no benefit in La'na it is a requirement of (the principle) 'Love for Allah's sake and Hate for Allah's sake.' (Maktoobaat)

Ala Hadrat, Imam of the Ahl e Sunnah, Molaana Shah Ahmad Riza Khan writes:

'The state of this filthy group, especially its leaders, is like that of the filthy Yazeed, upon him be whatever is upon him, in that the cautious have preferred silence over his kufr. The difference between Yazeed and their obstinate Imam is that Yazeed's fisq and oppression is proven with tawaatur but his kufr is not, whilst the words of kufr are narrated with tawaatur from these people.' (Al Kokaba As Shahaabiya)

He also writes :

'If anyone calls Yazeed a Kaafir we will not prevent him but we will not say it ourselves.' (Al Malfoodhaat)

In a third place he writes:

'That filthy (Yazeed) sent Muslim bin Uqba to the peaceful Madeenah and martyred 1700 great Muhaajireen, Ansaar and Tabi'een and subjected the people of Madeenah to lootings, killings and all types of tribulations. This vicious army stabled its horses in the Prophet's ﷺ masjid and did not allow anyone to pray there. They forcibly took a bai'a of enslavement from the people of the haram, meaning Yazeed could sell them or let them go free. Anyone who said that he was taking a bai'a upon the command of Allah and His Prophet ﷺ was killed. After having degraded the Prophet's ﷺ house they turned to degrade Allah's house. En route Muslim bin Uqba died and Husayn bin Nameer led the large army to Makkah and torched the Ka'ba and inflicted many and great sufferings and oppressions upon the inhabitants there.' (Ahsan ul Wa'aa p52).

In a fourth place, in response to the question **'What do the Ulama of the Ahl e Sunnah say, in light of the Quran and Sunnah, about Yazeed, will he be forgiven or not?'** he writes:

'There are three views of the Ulama of the Ahl e Sunnah about the filthy Yazeed:

1.   Imam Ahmad and other elders know him to be a kaafir and so will not be forgiven at all.

2.   Imam Gazaali etc call him a Muslim and (so) no matter how much he will be punished he will enviably be forgiven.

3. Our Imam (Abu Haneefa) remained silent and stated that we do not call him a Muslim but nor do we call him a Kaafir thus on this issue (of forgiveness) we will also stay silent. And Allah knows best.' (Ahkaam e Shariat)

In a fifth place he said in response to the question '*What do the ulama and jurists say about this issue that some people claim Yazeed was not a faajir or faasiq and should not be slandered whilst Imam Husayn should not have come out against him, why did he and this was (merely) a political war*'. He answers:

'Yazeed, upon him be from Allah whatever he is entitled to, definitely and undoubtedly is, with the ijma of the Ahl e Sunnah, a faasiq, faajir and committer of the gravest of sins.

There is the complete agreement and unanimity of the Imam's of the Ahl e Sunnah upon this. There is only disagreement over his Takfeer (apostasy) and La'na (damnation). Imam Ahmad bin Hanbal, his followers and his congruents call him a kaafir and perform La'na upon him by name. They use this verse as proof *'May it not be [the case] with you that if you were to turn away, you would then cause sedition in the land and sever your kinship ties?' (Quran 47:22)*. There is no doubting that after becoming ruler of the kingdom Yazeed spread discord on the Earth and severely violated the Haramain and in particular the Ka'ba and the tomb of the Prophet 爨; horses were stabled in the blessed masjid (of the Prophet 爨) and their faeces and urine defecated the blessed pulpit. For three days the masjid was without adhaan or prayer and thousands of Sahaaba were needlessly martyred in Makka, Madeenah and the Hijaaz. They stoned the Ka'ba, ripped its cloth and set it alight. He made the virtuous women of Madeenah halal for three days for his scum army. After keeping the Prophet's 爨 grandson without food or water for three days they mercilessly slaughtered him and his companions. And with their horses they trampled the delicate body that had been nurtured in the laps of the Prophet ﷺ. All the bones were crushed. The blessed head, which the Prophet ﷺ would kiss, was ripped off and stuck upon a spear and paraded. The honourable women of the Prophet's ﷺ family were taken prisoner and humiliatingly presented in this scum's court. What greater 'breaking relations' and 'discord on earth' could there be?

Whoever does not consider these '*maloon*' acts fisq and fujoor is *mal'oon* himself! The Quran has clearly sent Allah's la'na upon them, and so Imam Ahmad and his congruents perform la'na upon him. Our Imam ul Azam (Abu Haneefa) has out of caution remained silent upon his takfeer and la'na because although his fisq and fujoor is proven with Tawaatur his kufr is not to the same degree of certainty (beyond doubt), so when it is not permissible to attribute a major sin (kabeera) simply on a possibility, kufr is most definitely not allowed. And Tawbah (repentence) is acceptable until the final breath and there is no definitive proof of it not happening and this is the safest (path). However rejecting his fisq and fujoor and blaming the oppressed Imam is against the necessary principles of the Ahl e Sunnah and clear misguidance and heresy, indeed, such a thought cannot even be imagined from a heart containing the light of the Prophet's ﷺ love (verse). No doubt such a person is a rejected Nasibite and an enemy of the Ahl e Sunnah. There is no point in even shaking hands with such a misguided heretic for he has gone against the authentic statement and needlessly wandered into the Shari wilderness and hurt the feelings of a Muslim. He has through his words hurt the heart of Fatima Az Zahra, Ali al Murtaza and the Prophet ﷺ himself. Indeed he has hurt Allah. 'Indeed those who are injurious to God and His Messenger, God has cursed them in this world and the Hereafter, and has prepared for them a humiliating punishment.' (Quran 33:57)' (Irfaan e Shariat)

Sadr us Shariah Molaana Amjad Ali Sahib writes:

'The filthy Yazeed was a faasiq faajir undertaker of major sins. May Allah forbid, what comparison is their between him and the fragrance of the Prophet ﷺ Imam Husayn. Today the misled ask why we should get involved in their dispute for both are our princes. Those who spout such nonsense are worthy of Hell rejected Kharijites Nasabites. Indeed there are three statements of the Ulama of the Ahl e Sunnah regarding Yazeed's Kufr and Lana. Our Imam ul Azam's position is silence i.e. we do not call this faasiq and faajir either a kaafir or a Muslim.' (Bahaar e Shariah)

Take a look at a fatwa of Molvi Ashraf Ali Taanwi:

Question: Are the people of the Ahl e Sunnah, with regards to Imam Husayn, merely following the Shia? Is Imam Husayn's martyrdom only acknowledged after following the Shia or is there evidence of it in Shraiah because simply giving your life does not bring martyrdom, one must give one's life in pursuit of elevating the word of Allah. This kind of thing did not happen at Karbala, there Yazeed's army was merely trying to bring Imam Husayn under the rule of Yazeed and make him acknowledge Yazeed as the king. However Imam Husayn refused to accept Yazeed as the king and flatly refused (the questioner then continues with such similar points)?

Answer: Yazeed was a faasiq and the rule of a faasiq is a matter of disagreement. Some companions believe it was permissible whilst Imam Husayn deemed it impermissible. Even if it was permissible to subjugate oneself to Yazeed with dislike it was not compulsory and because Imam Husayn was attached to the truth (was in the right) he was oppressed and the murdered oppressed is a martyr. Martyrdom is not specific to battles. Based on this oppression we will deem him a martyr. In addition we do not absolve Yazeed from this killing because why was he trying to force a mujtahid (Imam Husayn) to follow him?! Especially at the end when Imam Husayn said he was not claiming anything. He (Yazeed) had enmity and this was the basis of Imam Husayn's killing. The permissibility of following a usurper is one matter but where is it permissible to usurp (power)!? Especially the unworthy! In fact it was wajib upon him to resign.' (Imdaad ul Fataaawa)

This fatwa of Ashraf Ali Taanvi is presented to reveal his thoughts on Yazeed because today some of his followers have adopted a very different opinion of Yazeed.

Molvi Rashid Ahmad Gangohi writes:

'Some of the Imams who have held their tongue regarding Yazeed's kufr (apostasy) have done so through caution (because) although knowing the murder of Imam Husayn as Halal is kufr it is not proven that Yazeed thought of this murder as Halal thus one should remain cautious in calling him a kaafir. However he is undoubtedly a faasiq.' (Fataawa Rashidiya)

In another place he writes:

'Yazeed's indecent acts are worthy of La'na. Whoever comes to know from definitive proofs and from the Quran that he was happy and in agreement with these *mufaasid* (corrupt) acts and deemed them good and permissible, and died without repenting, such a person is convinced of the permissibility of La'na upon him. And this is correct. And those ulama who have shown restraint in this (do so because) firstly he was a believer. After that it is not proven that he deemed these acts halal and without such evidence La'na is not permissible. Thus this group of ulama prevents La'na based on the hadith prohibiting La'na upon a Muslim and this point is also true. Consequently the permissibility or not of La'na depends on history and for us *Muqalideen* (of Imam ul Azam) caution is in silence because even if La'na was permissible there is no harm in not performing it because it is neither fard, nor wajib, nor sunnah nor Mustahab. It is only mubah (allowable) and it is not the place to involve oneself in sin.' (Fataawa Rashidiya)

Molvi Qasim Nanotvi, founder of the Dar ul Uloom Deoband writes:

'In summary, per the principles of the Ahl us Sunnah, Yazeed changed from his earlier condition. Some believe he became a kaafir whilst for others his kufr was not proven and instead his earlier Islam had become mixed with fisq. If Imam Husayn deemed him a kaafir then what was wrong with coming out against him? Imam Ahmad preferred this view. Thus it is possible that someone's being a kaafir is proven to one person and not to another. And similarly (and consequentially) there will be disagreement over coming out against him and it is not a religious requirement for there to be agreement (or unanimity) over *Takfeer, Tafseeq, Ta'deel* or *Tajreeh.*' (Maktoobaat Shaykh ul Islam)

Molvi Muhammad Tayyib writes :

'Nevertheless there is total agreement of all the companions upon Yazeed's fisq and fujoor, whether they supported him or opposed him. After them the Mujtahid Imams are also all agreed. Then after them the Raasikheen Ulama, Muhadditheen and Fuqaha such as Allaama Qustalaani, Alaama Badr ud Deen Aini, Allaama Haythami, Allaama Ibn Jowzi, Allaama Saad ud Deen Taftazaani, Muhaqiq Ibn Himaam, Hafiz Ibn Katheer and Allaama Kiyaa'alhiraasi, relate the unanimity of the Salaf Ulama upon Yazeed's fisq and they were also convinced of it themselves. So what greater proof of the unanimity of Yazeed's fisq can there be?!'

In a second place he writes:

'Put aside his fisq, some of the Imams even proceeded to discuss the matter of his Takfeer! Those who became aware of the states of his heart, mind and inner emotions went as far as calling him a kaafir. Although this is not the opinion of the majority it does at least necessarily reinforce and confirm his fisq.' (Shaheed e Karbala and Yazeed)

The Imam of the Ghair Muqallideen Nawab Siddiq Hassan writes :

'Ibn Abbaas states that during a siesta he saw the Prophet ﷺ in a dream, he was upset, his beard was wet and he was carrying a glass bottle filled with blood. I asked 'Yaa Rasoolallah what is this?' He replied 'It is the blood of Husayn and his companions, I am taking it to Allah' After a few days news arrived that on that day at that very time he (Imam Husayn) had been martyred (narrated by Bayhaqee). The people also heard the Jinn wailing over Husayn (as narrated by Abu Nuaim etc). Many have mentioned that when the blessed head was being taken to Yazeed they stopped at a temple for a siesta and found the following words scribed on the wall:

Does the nation that killed Husayn hope for his grandfather's intercession on the day of reckoning?
Maqrezi in Khatat narrates that when Imam Husayn was killed the sky cried. It is this crying that is the redness of the sky. Ata in the exegesis of the verse *'so neither the heaven nor the earth wept for them'* (Quran 44:29) has said 'its crying is the red of its sides'. Zuhri has said that it had reached him that on the day of Imam Husayn's murder no stone or rock was turned over in Jerusalem without fresh blood flowing from it and the world was in darkness for three days. Imam Husayn's camels were slaughtered and cooked but they all

became sour and no one was able to eat their meat. Blood rained from the sky and turned everything bloody. Zuhri also stated that no one from the killers of Imam Husayn survived and each was punished on this Earth before Akhirah; he was either killed, disgraced, physically deformed or his estate was destroyed over time.

The Grandson of Ibn Jowzee narrates that an old man had taken part in this battle and become blinded. When he was asked the reason (for his blindness) he revealed: 'I saw Imam Husayn in armour and a sword in his hand. There was a hard palate upon which lay the corpses of 10 men who had killed Imam Husayn, he sent La'na upon me and said bad things about me and threw a drop of blood into my eyes. When I awoke in the morning I was blind. The grandson of Ibn Jowzee also narrates 'One man hung the blessed head of Imam Husayn from the horse's neck and after a few days he became darker than tar and died in a very bad way. After hearing this event a man refused to believe it and fire flew at his body and burned him.'

Ibn Abbas narrates that Allah revealed to the Prophet ﷺ: 'I have killed 70,000 in recompense of Yahya bin Zakariyaa and in recompense of your grandson I have twice killed 70,000.' This is narrated by Haakim who authenticated it and Dhahabi in Takhlees said that it was upon the conditions of Muslim.

Hafiz Ibn Hajar with a weak chain narrates that Syeduna Ali said the murderers of Husayn are in a coffin of fire which receives half the punishment of the People of the Earth. Imam Suyooti in *Muhaadaraat wa Muhaawaraat* writes that in Kufa one year there was an outbreak of small pox and 1,500 children of those who were present and murdered Imam Husayn were blinded.

The details, based on sahih narrations, of Imam Husayn's martyrdom are written in the book *'Sirr us Shahaadatain'* and that should be referred to. There is disagreement in the La'na of Yazeed. For one group of scholars Yazeed's order and agreement to the murder of Imam Husayn is not proven and so they prohibit La'na upon Yazeed. Imam Gazaali and others lean towards this, they say that Iblis is Mal'oon (worthy of la'na) with Ijma but that does not require us to perform la'na upon him and nor is doing so an act of ibaada or good and the matter is between Yazeed and Allah. The other group of scholars who believe this act was Yazeed's own allow La'na. Imam Taftazaani is of this opinion and says: 'We will not show restraint regarding his acts nor even his iman, may Allah's La'na be upon him, his helpers and his supporters!' The prominent opinion is that silence is preferable to this activity.' (Tashreef ul Bashr Bi Dhikr Al Aima Al Ithna Ashar p49)

Abu'Ala Maududi, Ameer of Jamaat e Islami writes:

'Three events took place during the reign of Yazeed that shook the whole of the Islamic world:

The first event is of the martyrdom of Imam Husayn. Undoubtedly on the invitation of the people of Kufa he was on his way to overthrow Yazeed's government. And Yazeed's government saw him being in open rebellion. Let us for one moment put aside the question of whether or not on the principles of Islam Imam Husayn's stand was permissible, even though we do not find even one statement from any of the Sahaaba or Tabi'een, both in his lifetime or after it, claiming it to be impermissible and that he was on his way to undertake a haram activity. The companions that tried to stop him did so not because it was illegal but in light of prudence they did not see it as the best course of action. So even if we accept Yazeed's view as correct it is still a fact that Imam Husayn did not leave with an army, rather he was with his family and children; 32 mounted and 40 on foot. No one could ever call this an army on the march! To confront them the army sent from Kufa under Amar bin Sad bin Abi Waqaas numbered 4,000. There was no need for such a large army to have fought with this small group, it could easily have surrounded and arrested them all. especially in light of Imam Husayn's statement at the end when he demanded to be either allowed to return home, be sent to the frontier or be taken to Yazeed. However the army did not accept any of these and only offered to take him to Ubayd ullah bin Ziyaad, which Imam Husayn refused as he was well aware of what he had done to Muslim bin Aqeel earlier. Ultimately they attacked him and when all his companions had been martyred and Imam Husayn was left standing alone in the field they still saw it necessary to attack him and when he had fallen to the ground injured they butchered him. They then stole everything he had on his body, even his clothes, and then trampled his body with horses. After that the tents were looted and even the veils of the women were ripped off. After that all the martyrs of Karbala were beheaded and their heads taken to Ibn Ziyaad in Kufa. Not only did he display them publically but mounted the pulpit in the central masjid and declared 'Praise be to Allah who has revealed the Truth and the people of Truth, He has helped the Ameer of the believers Yazeed and his group and killed the lying son of the liar, Husayn ibn Ali, and his group.' The heads were then sent to Damascus where Yazeed displayed them in a full court. (For more details see Tibri, Ibn Al Atheer, Al Bidaaya wa Nihaaya)

If we, for a moment, do accept Yazeed's viewpoint that Imam Husayn was a rebel does Islam not provide rules for dealing with rebels? All the comprehensive books of 'Fiqh mention the rules, for example in the book Hidaaya and its shar Fath ul Qadeer we can look at the Chapter of Rebellion. In light of these rules each and every part of this episode from the plains of Karbala to Kufa and then the court in Damascus is undoubtedly haram (unlawful) and a severe crime. Regarding the events in Yazeed's court and what he said there are differing narrations, if we ignore all of them and just accept the authentic narration that on seeing the heads of Imam Husayn and his companions he became wet-eyed, and said 'I was happy with your service even without the killing of Husayn. May Allah's la'na be upon Ibn Ziyaad, by God if I had been there I would have forgiven Imam Husayn. O Husayn, had I been standing opposite you I would not have killed you' it raises the question of what punishment he gave his transgressing governor for this great crime (of killing Imam Husayn)? Hafiz Ibn Katheer states that he did not give him any punishment, nor did he remove him from his post, he did not even write a letter of condemnation to him! Had Yazeed even a spec of human dignity, let alone Islam for that is a higher state, he would have remembered how much favour the Prophet 🌙 had shown his family after the conquest of Makka and what his government had done to his grandson!

After this the second extremely painful event was the 'episode of Hurra' which took place at the end of both year 63 and Yazeed's life. The brief transcript of this episode is that the people of Madeenah declared Yazeed a faasiq, faajir and oppressor and revolted against him. After expelling his officers from the city they declared Abdullah bin Hanzala as their leader. On hearing this Yazeed sent Muslim bin Uqba Al Maree (whom the Salaf us Saaliheen called Musraf bin Uqba) with a 12,000 strong army to Madeenah and ordered him to give the people three days to accept his rule, if they did not accept he should fight them and after victory make the city 'halal' for his army for three days. Based on this guidance the army marched and a battle took place and Madeenah was overrun, then as per Yazeed's command the city was made permissible for the army for three days to do whatever it wished. During those three days they sacked everything and killed the inhabitants freely. According to Imam Zuhri 700 dignitaries (companions) and 10,000 ordinary people were killed. What was worse was that this barbaric army sneaked into the houses and violated the honour of the pure women of the city. Ibn Katheer states that it is narrated that 1,000 women became pregnant outside marriage during these days. (for more details of this episode see Tibri, Ibn Atheer and Al Bidaaya wa Nihaaya)

Even if we deem the revolt of the people of Madeenah as impermissible was what happened to them permitted under Islamic law for any revolting Muslim locality, or even a non Muslim rebel, or even a warring infidel?! What is more is that we are not discussing any ordinary city but the Prophet's very own city, about which he said, as narrated by Bukhaari, Muslim, Nisai, from countless companions :

'Whoever intends bad for the people of Madeenah Allah will dissolve him in the fire of Hell like lead' and 'Whoever hurts the people of Madeenah Allah will hurt him and upon him is the La'na of Allah, the Angels and all the people. On the day of Qiyaama Allah will not accept anything in compensation for his sins.'

Ibn Katheer states that based on these ahadith a section of the ulama have permitted La'na upon Yazeed and one statement of Imam Ahmad ibn Hanbal supports it too. However there is another section of the ulama that prevents La'na upon him on the basis that it could open the door of La'na upon his father and other companions. Once Syeduna Hassan Basri was taunted for not taking part in any stand against the Banu Umayya and so must be happy with the people of Shaam (i.e. the Banu Umayya)? He replied 'Am I pleased with the people of Shaam? May Allah destroy them, are they not those who made permissible the Prophet's 🌸 haram (sanctity) and for three days went about killing its inhabitants and allowed their barbaric soldiers to do what they wanted and they attacked the noble and pious ladies and left no sanctity unviolated. After that they marched on the House of Allah and showered it with stones it and set fire to it. May Allah's La'na be upon them and may they see a very dreadful end!' (Ibn ul Atheer)

The third event is the one which Imam Hasan Basri mentioned at the end, after finishing with Madeenah the same army, which ran riot in the Prophet's 🌸 haram, marched towards Makka to take on Ibn Zubayr. After setting up catapults they pelted the Ka'ba and damaged one of its walls. Even though there are narrations of them setting fire to the Ka'ba other explanations for the fire have also been narrated, however the stoning of the Ka'ba is an agreed matter.'

From all these narrations Yazeed's character, actions and status become as clear as daylight. All the Sahaaba, great Imams and grand scholars are unanimous in their view of Yazeed being a faasiq, faajir, tyrant and drunkard. There are however differing views about him being kaafir and worthy of La'na. Some have clearly declared him a kaafir and deemed it permissible to perform La'na upon him whilst others prevent it and stay silent; just as has been mentioned before. However to call Yazeed a scholar, learned, god fearing, extremely pious, prayer, faster, extremely kind and good natured etc is a complete lie and utterly false and without basis in reality. The only person who could have such a view and belief is the one with the sickness of hypocrisy and hatred for the Pure Ahl ul Bait.

Now take a look at the opinions of Yazeed held by his contemporaries from the Sahaaba and Ta'bieen:

The great companion Abdullah bin Hanzala, who was washed (given the funeral ghusl) by the Angels, narrates:

'By Allah, we did not come out against Yazeed until we feared stones would befall us from the sky for that man (Yazeed) allowed marrying mothers, daughters and sisters and would drink wine and miss the prayer.' (Tabaqaat Ibn Saad, Ibn Atheer)

Umar bin Sabiyya narrates:

'Yazeed undertook one Hajj during his father's lifetime. On arriving in Madeenah he organised a wine session. By chance Abdullah ibn Abbas and Imam Husayn passed by and asked to meet him. Ibn Abbas was not given permission but Imam Husayn was allowed in. When he entered he asked 'Glory be to Allah, What is this fragrance?' Yazeed replied 'This is the fragrance that originates from Shaam' and called for a glass of wine and drank from it. He then called for another and offered 'Drink O Abu Abdullah (Imam Husayn)' Imam Husayn scolded 'Keep your drink for yourself, I do not even want to look at it!' Yazeed then recited the following verses 'O friend, how strange! I invite you to pleasure and you refuse! The Arab chiefs orbit around young women, desires, merriment and sparkling drink. Amongst these charming women is the one your heart longs for, and yet you do not respond?!' Imam Husayn stood up and said 'Nay, O Son of Ameer Muaawiya, it has overcome your heart!' (Ibn Atheer)

Ibn Jowzee, Qurtubi and Tibraani narrate that after the tragedy of Karbala Yazeed appointed his cousin Uthman bin Muhammad bin Abu Sufyaan the governor of Madeenah and ordered him to force the people to take his Bai'a. Consequently after arriving in Madeenah he organised and sent a delegation of Madinites to take Yazeed's Bai'a.

Yazeed lavished upon them gifts and rewards but despite these

'When that delegation returned it revealed Yazeed's evil traits; on returning they declared that they had returned from a man who had no religion, who drank wine and played the guitar such that musicians were with him all the time signing and playing music. He played with dogs. We make you witness that we have broken our bai'a to him' ....
Abdullah bin Abu Umar bin Hafs Makhzoomi added 'Even though Yazeed has given me rewards and been good to me he is in truth the enemy of Allah and a drunkard. I leave his bai'a just as I take this turban off my head.' He then took of his turban. Another man said 'I come out of his bai'a like I come out of my shoe.' After him all the people did the same such that there was a pile of turbans and shoes.' (Wafaa ul Wafaa)

Munzar bin Zubair said openly before the people:

'No doubt Yazeed rewarded me with 100,000 Dhirham but his deed won't stop me telling you about him, By God, he drank wine and would become so drunk that he would miss the prayer.' (Ibn Atheer, Wafaa ul Wafa)

The Imam of the Awliyaa Imam Hasan Basri said:

'Ameer Muaawiya sought to make his son the Caliph after him who was a drunk, wine drinker, silk wearer and player the guitar.' (Ibn Atheer)

When Ameer Muaawiya decided to make Yazeed his heir he called people from all the cities and they all spoke in support of Yazeed. Yazeed bin Maqna alUzree said pointing to Ameer Muaawiya:

'This is Ameer ul Momineen and when he dies he will be (pointing to Yazeed) and if anyone denies it the sword will decide for him.' Ameer Muaawiya told him 'Sit down, you are the chief of the orators!' (Ibn ul Atheer)

Ameer Muaawiya then asked Ahnaf Bin Qais Basri, who was silent, what he thought, he replied:

'We fear you if we speak the truth and we fear Allah if we lie. O Ameer ul Momineen you know of Yazeed's nights and days, his hidden and his open, his inside and his outside. If you know him to be good for Allah and the Umma then there is no need for any consultation, but if you know him otherwise then do not make him an expediency for the duniya whilst you are travelling to the Akhirah. Nevertheless our duty is to say 'We hear and we obey.' Then a Syrian stood up and said 'We do not know what this subjugated Iraqi is saying! We have hearing and obedience but also the sword and the power!' (Ibn Atheer)

Muhammad bin Umar bin Hazm who had come from Madeenah said to Ameer Muaawiya:

'Every shepherd will be asked about his flock, look carefully at who you are leaving as your heir to the matters of the Umma of Muhammad.' On hearing this Ameer Muaawiya fall into a deep thought and kept his head bowed for a long while and his breath became heavy like on a winters day. He then rewarded him and sent him back'. (Ibn ul Atheer)

Ma'qal bin Sinaan was a very fierce critic of Yazeed because of the latter's unIslamic practices. When he was forcibly sent to Shaam to show support for Yazeed he said the following before Yazeed's closest courtier Muslim bin Aqba Musarrif:

'I have been sent here forcibly to take the bai'a of this man (Yazeed) and my coming here is nothing other than destiny and fortune. The man who drinks wine and marries women forbidden to him (how can I take his bai'a)!' He then mentioned all his evils and said 'O Musarrif, keep all this to yourself.' Musarrif said 'Today I will not mention this to the Ameer ul Momineen but I promise you that when I get the opportunity and I have you in my grasp I will hit you so hard your eyes will shut (will die).' (Tabqaat Ibn Saad)

Daynoori states that Ma'qal also added that on returning to Madeenah he would break the bai'a of this faasiq and faajir and give bai'a to one of the Muhaajireen.' (Akhbaar ul Atwaal)

Consequently he did as he had promised; when Abdullah bin Zubayr claimed the Caliphate in the Hijaaz he gave him his bai'a. Then during the event of the Hurra Muslim bin Uqba Musarrif came to Madeenah and killed and looted. Ma'qal was one of those arrested by Yazeed's army and was brought before Musarrif. Ma'qal was very thirsty and Musarrif asked:

'You appear thirsty' He replied 'Yes' so Musarrif had juice brought forward. After letting him drink it he said 'You will not now hope for anything refreshing' and ordered Nofal bin Musaahiq to rise and break his neck. In this way this companion of the Prophet 🌸 also became a victim of their oppression.' (Ibn Saad)

Look at what Yazeed's own companion Ibn Ziyaad thought of him: 'And Yazeed then ordered Ibn Ziyaad to march on Madeenah and lay siege to Ibn Zubayr in Makkah. Upon this Ibn Ziyaad protested 'By Allah I will not, for the sake of this faasiq, combine for myself the killing of the Prophet's 🌸 son (which he had already done) and fighting in the Ka'ba. He thus sent his apologies to Yazeed (i.e. refused to do as he was ordered).' (Ibn Atheer)

When news of Imam Husayn's murder reached Abdullah bin Zubayr he addressed the people. After the Praise and Glory of Allah and blessings and salutations upon the Prophet ﷺ he said:

'The people of Iraq, save for a very few, are all traitors and faajir, in particular the people of Kufa are extremely evil. They invited Imam Husayn and said they would support him and make him their leader but when Imam Husayn arrived they joined the enemy and attacked him and told him that he could either give himself up to them, so they could send him to Ibn Ziyaad bin Sameed who could decide what to do with him, or he could fight them! Imam Husayn saw that he and his companions were few whilst his opponents were great in number, but despite this the Imam rejected a life of humiliation for dying with honour! May Allah have mercy upon him and may He humiliate his murderer. By my life, the disobedience the people of Iraq showed and their treachery in joining the enemy is sufficient counsel for others and enough for them to stay wary of the people of Iraq. Whatever is destined ultimately takes place and when Allah decides on a matter it cannot be stopped. Can we ever be content with the people of Iraq and see them as truthful after Imam Husayn's event? And ever accept their promises? By Allah, no. We do not deem them worthy of this; By Allah they have indeed killed a man (Imam Husayn) who stood all night (in prayer) and fasted all day, who had more right in this matter (government) than them and was much better than them in his deen, his virtue and his rank. By Allah he was not of those who spread misguidance in stead of the Quran. There was no limit to his crying and pleading in fear of Allah, he did not replace his fasts with wine drinking and nor did his gatherings contain the discussion of hunting dogs in place of the Dhikr of Allah - he said all these matters about Yazeed - and very soon these people will enter the *Gayy* valley of Hell.'

He also mentioned Yazeed's defects:

'Yazeed was famous for wine drinking, playing with dogs and bringing the deen into disrepute.' (Hayaat ul Haiwaan)

As for Muhammad bin Hanfiya staying with Yazeed and testifying to his prayers, piety, scholarliness and strict adherence to the Sunnah, its simple answer is that it is not supported by any sound narration, even when Ibn Katheer quoted it he did so without any narration, meaning it is unreliable.

Once in the court of the Umayyad Caliph Umar bin Abdul Aziz a man referred to Yazeed as Ameer ul Momineen. Umar bin Abdul Aziz became furious and protested:

'You call Yazeed Ameer ul Momineen?!' and ordered the man to be whipped twenty times as punishment. (Tahzeeb ul Tahzeeb)

WHY SOME COMPANIONS ACCEPTED YAZEED?

- *If Yazeed was truly a faasiq, faajir, oppressor, drunkard etc then what of the companions who took his bai'a?*

- *Why did they uptake his bai'a?*

- *Are they not guilty of entering the bai'a of a faasiq and faajir?*

- *If they are not, then why did Imam Husayn refuse his bai'a and take a stand against him?*

These types of questions effectively meant that if Imam Husayn was right then the companions who entered into his bai'a must have been wrong and guilty of fisq, but if those companions were right then Imam Husayn must have been wrong to stand against him and thus guilty of rebellion.

The answer to these questions is that the companions who took the bai'a of Yazeed were upon the truth and Imam Husayn was also upon the truth. Neither is blameworthy because both acted upon the Pure Shariah. This is explained by the fact that the commands of Shariah are of two types; those based on Expediency (Rukhsa) and those based on 'Azeema.

For example if one is caught in the claws of an oppressor or disbeliever and is being compelled with threats of all kinds of evil (death, rape, loss of property etc) to commit heresy (e.g. renege on the testimony of faith etc) then if the Muslim genuinely believes these threats will be carried out against him if he refuses and will be spared if he utters words of heresy then in this desperate situation the Shariah has allowed him to utter the words of heresy to save himself, as long as, in his heart, he does not believe in them and is steadfast upon the truth. This is what is known as Rukhsa (expediency) and because Shariah has allowed him to do this and by doing so he has acted within the commands of Shariah there can be no reproach or blame upon him. If we were to blame him that would merely be our own ignorance. However if that Muslim had remained steadfast and withstood the evil and torture of the oppressor and not allowed his tongue to utter heresy such that he was killed he would be known as a martyr and *mujaahid*, indeed Shariah has deemed this the greatest Jihad. This is what is known as 'Azeema and is better than Rukhsa. So we do not have any right to reproach anyone who has undertaken this great jihad in line with the commandments of Shariah. If we do it will only be our own foolishness.

Those companions who took Yazeed's bai'a according to this principle of Shariah did not do so because they believed he was a rightful Caliph or a just Imam but did so to be spared fighting, discord, sedition and his oppression and evil. They acted upon Rukhsa. Allaama Ibn Khuldun writes 'When the matters of fisq occurred in Yazeed, which occurred in him, the companions were in disagreement over what to do. Some deemed it necessary to stand against him and break his bai'a, like what Imam Husayn, Abdullah bin Zubair and others did. (On the other hand) There were those who refused to take a stand based on the fear of fitna and great killings. This was because at that time Yazeed's strength and honour was the pride of the Banu Umayya.' (Muqaddima Ibn Khuldun)

This text proves that those companions who took Yazeed's bai'a and did not stand against him did so not because he was a rightful Caliph or a just imam but did so to prevent sedition, killings and discord. They knew that if this fire of fitna was lit it would be very difficult to contain and so acted upon 'Rukhsa'.

On the other hand Imam Husayn stood firm upon the Truth and Imaan and made a stand against him, in the course of which he withstood great and endless evils at the hands of the Yazeedites and ultimately sacrificed his own and his companions lives. However he never took a backward step. His course of action was based on 'Azeema', he undertook the greatest Jihaad and is thus the grandest Mujaahid and greatest martyr.

Had Imam Husayn not done this how would the practice of Azeema have been established?! Whose resolve and sacrifice could forthcoming brave men and women have used as an example of standing fast upon the truth and facing up to tyrants and oppressors?! Whose remembrance would have been companion and source of strength in their most testing of times?! And how else would we have known that this too was also a form of victory and honour?!

Similarly on the other hand if this example of Rukhsa had not been established who would the coming generations of muslims who wanted to remain steadfast upon the deen but lacking the strength to stand up to tyrants or oppressors or wanting to prevent bloodshed and discord have used as an example of Rukhsa?!

It is for this reason that the Prophet ﷺ said 'My companions are like the stars, following them is guidance' whether it be 'Azeema or Rukhsa. However as 'Azeema is the better of the two acting upon it will be the better option.

Consequently Imam e Ahl Sunnah Molaana Ahmad Rida Khan writes 'Here there were two scenarios, through fear of life to take the damned bai'a of accepting Yazeed's rule, even if it was against the Quran and Sunnah. This was Rukhsa and there was no reward in it. The other scenario was to give one's life and not take the bai'a of that impure. This was Azeema and upon it great reward, and it was the most appropriate (act) for his (Imam Husayn's) high status and that is what he chose.' (Al Hujja t'ul Mutaminna Fi Ayaat Mutahinna)

Evidence for Rukhsa

Syeduna Oaf bin Malik As Shajee narrates that the Prophet ﷺ said:

'Be aware, whoever has a *Waali* (ruler) over him and sees in him a matter from the disobedience of Allah must dislike it but must not withdraw his hand from obedience.' (Muslim. Mishkaat)

Salama bin Yazeed Ja'fee narrates that the Prophet ﷺ was asked:

'O Prophet ﷺ of Allah, how do you see it if we have rulers over us who demand their right from us but hold back our rights, what do you order us (in this situation)?' He said 'Listen and obey (them) for verily upon them is their burden (of deeds) and upon you is your burden (of deeds).' (Muslim, Mishkaat)

Abdullah bin Masood narrates that the Prophet ﷺ said to us:

'Verily after me you will experience the unworthy being favoured and (you will experience) disliked matters.' The companions asked 'So what do you order us Yaa Rasoolallah?' He said 'Give them their rights and seek your rights from Allah?' (Bukhaari, Mishkaat)

Abu Zar narrates that the Prophet ﷺ asked him:

'How will you be when after me rulers will unlawfully take from the booty?' I replied 'By the One who sent you with the truth I would put my sword over my shoulder and keep striking it until I meet you (in Qiyaama)'. The Prophet ﷺ said 'Shall I not tell you of something better than that?! That you be patient until you meet me.' (Abu Dawud, Mishkaat)

Hudayfa bin Al Yamaan narrates that the Prophet ﷺ said:

'After me there will be rulers who will not act in (line with) my guidance, and not practice my sunnah and amongst them will be men whose hearts will be the hearts of the devil in human bodies.' I asked 'Yaa Rasoolallah, what should I do if I find such?' The Prophet ﷺ replied 'Listen and obey, even if they strike you on your back and take your property, listen and obey.' (Muslim)

Hudayfa narrates:

'I asked 'Yaa Rasoolallah, will there be evil after this goodness (of Islam that we now have) like there was before?' He said 'Yes' I asked 'What will be the salvation (from it)?' He said 'The sword (i.e. fighting).' I asked 'And will there be any (bad) left after the sword?' He said 'Yes, the Government will be established in the wrong way, people will not accept it with their hearts and it will be forced upon them.' I asked 'What will happen then?' He said 'People will call towards misguidance, if at that time you have a Caliph obey him, even if he whips you on your back and takes your wealth, obey him, if not go and die in a hole under a tree.' (Mishkaat)

Abdullah bin Umar narrates that the Prophet ﷺ said ;

'The ruler is Allah's shade on the Earth, all His oppressed servants run towards him. If he dispenses justice for him is reward and upon the people is gratitude and if he undertakes evil and oppression for him is the burden and upon the people is patience' (As Siraaj ul Muneer Fi Shar Jaame as Sageer)

Evidence for 'Azeema

Abu Saeed Khudri narrates that the Prophet ﷺ said:

> 'The best Jihad is (for) the one who speaks the word of truth before an oppressive king.' (Tirmidhi, Abu Dawud, Ibn Majah, Mishkaat)

Ka'b bin Ujza narrates that the Prophet ﷺ said to him :

> 'O Ka'b bin Ujza, I place you in Allah's refuge from the rule of the fools.' I pleaded 'Yaa Rasoolallah, what is the rule of the fools?' He said 'Soon will come rulers who when they speak will lie and when they act will oppress. So whoever will come and validate their lies and aid them in their oppression will not be from me and I will not be from him and tomorrow (on qiyaama) he will not come to my fountain (of Al Kawthar). And whoever will not go to them and will not validate their lies and will not aid them in their oppression will be from me and I from him and tomorrow (on qiyaama) he will come to my fountain.' (Kanz ul Ammaal)

Remember here the status of Imam Husayn; the Prophet ﷺ said 'Husayn is from me and I am from Husayn'. In this above hadith the Prophet ﷺ declares that the one who confirms and supports such rulers 'is not from me' so how could Imam Husayn have confirmed and supported them for he would no longer have remained 'Husayn is from me.' Consequently Imam Husayn only did what was required and befitted his rank and status.

Khalid narrates that they heard from the Prophet ﷺ:

> 'Verily when people see the tyrant and do not grab his hand (to stop him) it is near that Allah will make general upon them his punishment' (Abu Dawud)

Umar bin Hayshim narrates that the Prophet ﷺ said:

'There is no nation in which evil takes place and those with the power to change it do not except that soon Allah will make general his punishment upon them.' (Abu Dawud)

Hudayfa bin Al Yamaan narrates that the Prophet ﷺ said:

'The people of tyranny and their helpers are in Hell.' (Al Mustadrak)

Abu Saeed Khudri narrates that the Prophet ﷺ said :

'Whoever from you sees an evil should change it with his hand. If he does not have the ability he should (change it) with his tongue and if he does not have the ability he should (dislike it) with his heart and that is the weakest of Iman.' (Mishkaat)

How could the one; from whose household the fountain of Iman, guidance, piety and goodness flowed and through which the nation was purified; whose grandfather, after withstanding greats trials and tribulations, eradicated evil and promoted goodness; have allowed evil to come into being? How could he have witnessed evil and not tried to change it? Surely he had the greatest responsibility to take action, especially when his hand had (assumingly) been strengthened; his tongue had the ability and he undoubtedly reflected the Prophet's ﷺ bravery and courage! He heard the call of the time and had he not answered and not stepped forward to cleanse the nation the pure fountain of iman, guidance, goodness and piety would have become polluted and impure. He made a sincere resolve and every particle of Karbala is witness that he did what befitted his rank and status.

The sermon Imam Husayn delivered before Yazeed's army testifies to this and authenticates this claim. After the praise and eulogy of Allah Imam Husayn said :

'O People, verily the Prophet ﷺ said 'Whoever sees an

oppressive ruler making halal the things made haram by Allah, breaking the promises made to Allah, contradicting the Sunnah of the Prophet 🕮, dealing with Allah's people with sin and oppression and does not change it with actions or words as far as his ability allows Allah has the right to enter him into the ruler's place (of Hell). Be aware! Those people have made it necessary to follow the devil and to forsake the obedience of Allah, they will spread fisaad, and surpass the *hudood* (boundaries) of Allah, and spend the booty upon themselves, and made Halaal the Haraam (made by) of Allah and made Haraam what Allah made Halaal. Thus I have a greater right than any other person (to take a stand) and I also have your letters and messengers taking my bai'a and promising not to allow any harm to come to me and not to forsake me, so if you stay upon my Bai'a you will find guidance. I am Husayn the son of Ali, the son of Fatima the daughter of the Prophet 🕮.' (Ibn Atheer)

He then recited the following verses:

I will soon pass away but death is not a slight on the brave
Whilst his intentions are good and he is striving as a Muslim

The one who has followed the pious men
And opposed the destroyers and separated from the criminals

If I live I will be regretful and If I die there is no sorrow
For you is enough disgrace that you shall live in shame and humiliation

Undoubtedly he did only what befitted his high rank, and why would he not have done so when he was the very reflection of the Prophet's 🕮 courage and bravery. When the Prophet 🕮 was in his final illness Syeda Fatima took her two princes to the Prophet 🕮 and pleaded that they were his children and that he should bequeath them something.

The Prophet ﷺ said 'For Hassan is my awe and chieftain and for Husayn is my courage and generosity.' (Tibraani in Kabeer, Kanz ul Ammaal)

Ibn Asaakir mentions another narration:

'To Hassan I give me my chiefdom and my awe and to Husayn I give my bravery and compassion.'

Another narration of Ibn Asaakir is:

'To the eldest I give my awe and my grace and to this young one I give my love and my contentment.'

Glory be to Allah, both of these princes proved the virtues they received from the Prophet ﷺ; Imam Hassan was unique in his grace and patience whilst Imam Husayn showed such bravery, courage, love and contentment that we await another example of it. When the Prophet ﷺ never succumbed to falsehood how could the one who was the reflection of his courage and bravery bow down before falsehood!?

Furthermore the narration in which Imam Husayn asked to be taken to Yazeed so he could give his hand into his hand (and take his bai'a) is not correct. Uqba bin Sumaan narrates that he accompanied Imam Husayn from Madeena to Makka and then to Iraq and stayed with him until his martyrdom and heard the whole speech he made to the people on the day of his martyrdom:

'By Allah, He never said to the people that he would give his hand in Yazeed's hand and nor that he be taken to the frontier lands. Rather he asked to be let go and allowed to return from where he had come or to go anywhere else in this long and wide Earth so that all could see to whom the people give this matter (of government). However they did not agree to any of it.' (Ibn Atheer)

Abdullah bin Masood narrates that the Prophet ﷺ said:

'Soon you will have over you rulers who will delay the prayer and invent new matters (contrary to the Sunna).' Ibn Masood asked 'So how do I deal with it?' He said 'O Son of Umm e Abd, You ask me how to deal them?! There is no obedience of the one who disobeys Allah.' (Al Fath ul Kabeer)

Ubaada bin Saamit narrates that the Prophet ﷺ said:

'After me soon there will be rulers over you who will order you matters you do not recognise and do things you do not like, their obedience is not upon you.' (As Siraaj ul Muneer)

Abu Salaala Aslama narrates that the Prophet ﷺ said:

'Soon there will be rulers over you who will own your livelihoods, will speak to you and lie, will undertake evil and will not be pleased with you until you praise their evil and validate their lies. So present the truth before them until they allow you to and when they exceed it the one killed by them will be a martyr.' (As Siraaj ul Muneer)

In light of this narration Imam Husayn is undoubtedly a martyr, indeed he is the chief of the martyrs, as described below:

Jaabir narrates that the Prophet ﷺ said:

'Hamza bin Abdul Muttalib is the Chief of the martyrs and so is the man who stands up to a tyrannical ruler, commands him to do good and prohibits him from evil and is so killed.' (Al Mustadrak, As Siraaj ul Muneer)

Praise be to Allah, these reliable sources prove that there can be no kind of blame upon those companions who undertook the bai'a of Yazeed. This is because they acted upon Shariah's ruling of 'Rukhsa'. Similarly there is no type of blame upon Imam Husayn for he acted upon Shariah's command of 'Azeema. Acting upon 'Azeema is best and its reward is grand, and so his rank is very high, elevated and grand.

May Allah be pleased with them all.

YAZEED WAS NOT RESPONSIBLE
FOR THE KILLINGS?

There is a claim made that Yazeed did not order the killing of Imam Husayn and did not agree with it. As a result he should not be blamed for the martyrdom of Imam Husayn.

This claim is wrong. Yazeed did order the killing of Imam Husayn and was happy with it. Allaama Saad ud Deen Taftazaani, the author of Shara ul Aqaaid, writes:

> 'The truth is that Yazeed's agreement to the killing of Imam Husayn and his happiness over it, and his degradation of the Prophet's ﷺ Ahl ul Bait, are matters proven in meaning with *Tawaatur*, even though the details of them are *Ahaad* (single authentic narrations)'. (Shara ul Aqaaid An Nasafee)

Shaykh Muhaqqiq Shah Abdul Haque Muhaddith Dehlvi writes :

> 'Some say that Yazeed did not order the killing of Imam Husayn, nor was he happy with it and nor after the murder of Imam Husayn and his companions was he pleased and happy. This claim is rejected and is false. This is because this misfortunate's enmity with the Prophet's ﷺ Ahl ul Bait

and his rejoicing over their murder and humiliating them has reached the rank of Tawaatur in terms of meaning and refuting it is a Takalluf and Mukaabira i.e. is just making an issue for the sake of it!' (Takmeel ul Imaan)

The statements of these two great elders should be enough to dispel any doubts in this matter. However we will also provide evidence from the testimony of Yazeed's own appointed governor of Kufa and main representative during this whole tragic episode, the evil Ibn Ziyaad.

After Yazeed's death Ibn Ziyaad left for Shaam and en route fall into deep reflection. His travelling companion Musaafir bin Shareeh asked:

'Are you feeling sleepy?' He replied 'No, I was just thinking about something.' Musaafir bin Shareeh asked 'Shall I tell you what you were thinking about?' He said 'Tell me' He explained 'You were thinking if only I had not killed Imam Husayn.' Ibn Ziyaad protested 'As for the killing of Imam Husayn Yazeed ordered me to kill him or be killed so I chose killing Imam Husayn.' (Ibn Atheer)

Furthermore when after the killing of Imam Husayn Madeenah and Makkah rose up Yazeed ordered Ibn Ziyaad to march on Madeenah and besiege Ibn Zubayr in Makkah Ibn Ziyaad said:

'By Allah I will not, for the sake of this faasiq, combine for myself the killing of the Prophet's ﷺ son and fighting in the Ka'ba.' He thus sent his apologies to Yazeed (i.e. refused to do as he was ordered). (Ibn Atheer)

After Imam Husayn's martyrdom the cities of Makkah and Madeenah rose up in protest and accepted Abdullah bin Zubayr as their Caliph. However Abdullah ibn Abbas did not do so. On hearing this Yazeed assumed Ibn Abbas supported him and opposed Ibn

Zubayr and so wrote to Ibn Abbas:

'I learn that you have rejected Ibn Zubayr's bai'a and thereby remained upon my bai'a and shown loyalty. You should strongly encourage others to also show loyalty to me (Yazeed) and oppose Ibn Zubayr for you are someone people listen to and accept. I will not forget this show of loyalty and favour and will repay it.'

In response Ibn Abbas wrote back saying:

'By God I have not refused Ibn Zubayr's bai'a to keep you happy or seek reward from you, the reason for my refusal is well known to Allah. Do you reckon that in hope of your reward and favour I will invite people to befriend you and create hatred for Ibn Zubayr and force them to leave him? I will never do this and how can I do this for verily you killed Husayn and the youth of Abdul Muttalib, who were the leading lights and shining stars of guidance. Upon your orders your army turned them into dust and blood in a single place. They were martyred in a state of extreme thirst and their bodies lay unshrouded in the open whilst the wind blew dust upon them and the wild animals sniffed their bodies. Then eventually a nation that had nothing to do with their murder was given the ability by Allah to shroud and bury them all. Even if I sit in your court and find worldly honour I have not forgotten the matter and nor will I of how you forced Imam Husayn out of the Prophet's ﷺ haram of Madeenah to Allah's Haram in Makkah and then kept sending messengers to him by foot and by conveyance until you also forced him out of there to Iraq. Consequently he left Makkah in fear. Then your army, based on your enmity of Allah, His Prophet ﷺ and the Prophet's ﷺ Ahl ul Bait, whom Allah had cleansed of all intrinsic and extrinsic pollution and made pure and clean, surrounded them. Imam Husayn tried to reach an agreement with you and asked to be allowed to return home, but you saw his few helpers and this an opportune moment to destroy the Ahl ul Bait and helped one another attack them like as if you were attacking some Turk or disbelieving family! How strange it is that you hope for my friendship when you have killed my father's children and my blood is still dripping from your sword!? You are the murderer of my relatives. Do not be joyful or arrogant because you have overwhelmed us today for undoubtedly one day we will indeed be victorious over you!' (Ibn Atheer)

Consequently Ibn Katheer said:

'Undoubtedly Yazeed made a very grave mistake in his order to Muslim bin Uqba to give his army the freedom of Madeenah for three days. This was another grave criminal mistake to add (to his other mistakes) for it led to the killing of a great number of companions and their offspring. It has already been mentioned that he had Imam Husayn and his companions killed at the hands of Ibn Ziyaad. Verily in those three days many great vices were on display in the city of the Prophet ﷺ which (are so shameful that they) cannot even be mentioned or described; only Allah knows them well. By sending Muslim bin Uqba to Madeenah Yazeed had hoped his monarchy and government would be given strength and longevity and to which there would be no more challenges or disputes. However Allah punished him for his intention and did not allow what he had hoped for and destroyed him in the way He destroys tyrants and oppressors. Allah took hold of him too with His Powerful Perfect Strength and your Lord's taking hold is like that, like He took hold of the oppressive cities before. Very His taking hold is extremely painful.' (Al Bidaaya wa Nihaaya)

By looking closely at Ibn Katheer's words of displeasure it becomes clear that Imam Husayn's murder took place with the agreement and command of Yazeed.

After viewing the statements of Ibn Ziyaad, who was only made the governor of Kufa to destroy Imam Husayn's influence upon its people and was allowed to do whatever he needed to achieve this, and the statements of the great companion Abdullah bin Abbas; the Imam of the Ahl us Sunnah Allaama Taftazaani in Shara ul Aqaaid an Nasafee and Allaama Hafiz Ibn Katheer, any suspicions that the murder of Imam Husayn did not take place on the order and agreement of Yazeed and that he is of no blame for the tragic events of Karbala should be firmly extinguished.

Even the most simplest of minds can understand that no army officer or regional governor can kill an extremely important person of the land without the command and agreement of the highest authority. Thus the murder of the most notable members of the Prophet's 🌺 family; Imam Husayn and his relatives and companions, could not have been the unilateral action of any army officer or regional governor.

The truth is that all of this happened with the agreement and upon the command of Yazeed and the full responsibility of it falls upon him. There is an example of this in the Quran; Firawn did not personally kill any sons of the Bani Israeel but Allah in the Quran declared him as their killer for they were killed on his command. It is stated in the Quran {*'slaughtering your [newborn] sons and keeping your females alive}' (2:49)* this reveals that on whosoever's command a murder takes place he will be deemed the murderer. Thus it is wrong to say that Yazeed did not agree to the murder of Imam Husayn and that he did not give the command to murder him. Undoubtedly all of this took place upon the command and for the pleasure of the wretched Yazeed.

WAS YAZEED REMORSEFUL?

If Imam Husayn's murder took place on Yazeed's command and with his agreement why did he perform La'na upon Ibn Ziyaad and show remorse over the death of Imam Husayn? Surely he should have revealed his pleasure?!

Yazeed was happy but he did also perform La'na upon Ibn Ziyaad and show regret!

He was happy because the person who was the greatest threat to his rule and government was no more, and because of this his reckoning and respect for Ibn Ziyaad increased. Had he deemed the murder of Imam Husayn impermissible and Ibn Ziyaad a tyrant and worthy of La'na he should have sought retribution from him and punished him?! He could at least have removed him from his post. He did none of this! Proving that in his heart was joy for his objective had been achieved.

However he also knew that his forehead now the bore the dark mark of the unjust murder of Imam Husayn and the whole Islamic world would rebuke him until Qiyaamah. For only this fear of his impending condemnation did he show regret and sadness and performed verbal La'na upon Ibn Ziyaad. Thus this regret and La'na should only be seen as customary or political. Have a look at Ibn

Katheer's testimony supporting this claim:

'After Ibn Ziyaad had killed Imam Husayn and his companions and sent their heads to Yazeed he was at first pleased and his reckoning of Ibn Ziyaad's rank and position rose. However he did not remain happy for long and later became remorseful.' (Al Bidaaya wa Nihaaya)

Allaama Shaykh Muhammad bin Ali AlSibaan writes:

'Then he (Ibn Ziyaad) sent it (Imam Husayn's head) with his Ahl ul Bait, which included Imam Zain ul Abideen and his paternal auntie Syeda Zaynab, to Yazeed. Yazeed was overjoyed and made them stand where prisoners stood and humiliated them and played with and hit the honourable head with the stick he had with him and kept saying 'O Husayn you have met the fruits of your rebellion' and he was extravagant in his joy. He then became remorseful because the Muslims would despise him for it and the whole world would hate him.' (Isaaf ur Raagibeen)

These narrations clearly prove that at first Yazeed was happy over the murder of Imam Husayn but his joy did not last long as he soon realised and feared his impending ignominy and this made him sorry. This remorse was not over the murder of Imam Husayn but for his own humiliation. Listen to Yazeed's own words:

'May Allah's La'na be upon he son of Marjaana (Ibn Ziyaad) who tormented and forced Imam Husayn to come out, even though Imam Husayn had asked him to let him go anywhere to bring him to me or allow him to be sent to the frontier where he could spend his life undertaking Jihad. However Ibn Marjaana did not accept any of these and killed him and through his murder made me detestable for the Muslims and created in their hearts hatred and enmity for me. Now every good and bad will hate me for my killing of Husayn and it will be difficult and hurtful for the people. What have I with Ibn Marjaana, may Allah humiliate and destroy him.' (Al bidaaya wa Nihaaya)

Study carefully the final passage of Yazeed's words 'now every good and bad will hate me for my killing of Husayn'. With these he clearly admits that he is the murderer of Imam Husayn for everything happened upon his command. As for his La'na upon Ibn Ziyaad, it was not because he was unhappy with the murder of Imam Husayn, because that actually increased Ibn Ziyaad's standing and status with Yazeed, as mentioned before, rather it was because of his own impending humiliation which he was to encounter and did. Consequently Allaama Ibn Katheer declared:

'Verily Yazeed performed La'na upon Ibn Ziyaad because of his actions and swore at him because of what was to happen and begin (the people's hatred for him etc) however he did not remove him from his position or punish him or even send him a letter of admonishment.' (Al Bidaaya wa Nihaaya)

It is stated that Imam Gazaali prevented La'na upon Yazeed:

Imam Gazaali states:

'The acts that necessitate La'na are of three; *Kufr, Bid'a* and *Fisq*. Furthermore there are three levels of La'na for each of these three types; La'na with the general attribute for example saying 'Allah's La'na upon the Kaafireen, or Mubtadi'een or Fusaqaa.' The second type of La'na is with a specific attribute such as saying 'Allah's La'na upon the Yahood, or Nasaara, or Majoos, or Khwaarij, or Rawaafidh, or fornicators, or usurers etc'. Both of these types of La'na are permissible. However there is hesitation in La'na upon the People of Bid'a as it is difficult to recognise Bid'a. The third type is specific or personalised La'na and this is dangerous even for a kaafir, faasiq or mubtade, for example saying 'Allah's Lana upon Zaid'. It is also similarly dangerous for doing so upon anyone from our time, even if he is a kaafir etc, for example Lana upon Zaid who is a Yahoodi.' This is not good because he may have repented before death and become a Muslim.'

He further adds:

'In summary, there is danger in performing La'na upon specific people so one should refrain from it, whilst there is no danger in silence, (even in la'na upon Iblis! so there is even more danger for people other than him). So if it is asked whether La'na upon Yazeed is permissible because he killed Imam Husayn or ordered it, we respond that both of these items are not categorically proven.'

He further adds:

'And if it is asked if it is permissible to say 'Lana of Allah upon the murderer of Imam Husayn' or 'upon the one who ordered the killing of Imam Husayn' we would respond that the correct position is 'La'na upon the murderer of Imam Husayn if he died before repenting' for it is possible he may have died after repenting. For example Wahshee killed Ameer Hamza, the uncle of the Prophet ﷺ, whilst he was a disbeliever and then repented from disbelief and kufr so La'na upon him is not permissible. Killing is a major crime but is not kufr, thus when La'na is not restricted to repentance and is general there is danger, whilst there is no danger is silence. We have mentioned Yazeed here because people are very quick to employ their tongue in performing La'na whilst the believer is not one who performs La'na thus he should not open his tongue in La'na except upon the disbeliever who died upon kufr. And if he must perform

La'na he should not do so on a specific person but use a general description as mentioned above. Even better than that is if someone instead performs the Dhikr of Allah, and if he cannot do that he should remain quiet for there is safety in that ...... A man once asked the Prophet ﷺ to counsel him, he replied ' I advise you not to be one who performs La'na a lot.' (Ihya ul Uloom)

Imam Gazaali has mentioned all this as part of his discussion of the trials and tribulations of the tongue and discussed performing La'na excessively along with other ills such as frivolous talk, excessive talking, talking about evil, quarrelling, swearing, mocking and jest, lying, backbiting etc.

Imam Gazaali has stated that it is permissible to perform La'na upon disbelievers and misguided sects such as the Khawaarij etc but has prevented La'na upon a specific person for it is dangerous. This is through utmost caution and is proof of the highest degree of Taqwa (piety). Look at his words again 'It is not good to perform La'na upon a specific contemporary person, even if he is kaafir,' he also states that there is no harm if one doesn't even perform La'na upon the devil. Is there anyone more worthy of it than the devil?!

The strange thing is that those who use this statement of Imam Gazaali to prevent Lana upon Yazeed themselves spend day and night slandering Muslims of Shirk and Bid'a!

Imam Gazaali has said it is not good to perform La'na upon a specific kaafir because he may repent even though the Quran has said 'Allah's La'na upon the disbelievers' and also that one should not perform La'na upon Iblis and stay quiet even though every Muslim declares every day 'I seek Allah's refuge from the Cursed Devil' so those who present this quote of Imam Gazaali should also consider the disbelievers and the cursed devil not worthy of La'na. Do these people not know the difference between someone being 'worthy of La'na' and 'performing La'na upon him.' Imam Gazaali's purpose was that in light of the ahadith a believer is not one who performs La'na i.e. even if someone is worthy of La'na the believer does not perform La'na upon him. The proof of this is that according to Imam Gazaali La'na using a general description is permissible, such as the kaafir, faasiq, khwaarij, fornicator, usurer, and tyrant. Yazeed was undoubtedly a faasiq and faajir so according to Imam Gazaali's principle La'na upon him is permissible, but without mentioning his name. And this is only because according to him he did not permit the murder of Imam Husayn and that he may have repented.

We have proven from the great Imams and Ulama that Imam Husayn's murder was undertaken on his command and with his agreement. Abdullah bin Abbas also deemed Yazeed the murderer and wrote a letter to him telling him that he was the murder of Husayn and the children of Abdul Muttalib. Furthermore even the cursed Ibn Ziyaad admitted and declared that he killed Imam Husayn on the order of Yazeed. Thus La'na is permissible upon Yazeed if and when it is proven that he killed or ordered the killing of Imam Husayn

OTHER MISCONCEPTIONS

1) It is claimed that some scholars praised Yazeed

In response to this it must be noted that all the great scholars have rejected any writings in praise of Yazeed. For example Ibn Kathir writes 'As Shaykh Abdul Mugeeth bin Zuheer Al Harbi was from the pious of the Hanbalites and would receive visitations from the people. He wrote a book in praise of Yazeed in which he mentioned many strange and weird things. Allaama Abu'l Farj Ibn al Jawzi refuted this book and produced a very excellent and correct refutation.' (Al bidaaya wa Nihaaya)

2) Allaama Ibn Kathir praised Yazeed

Some misquote Ibn Kathir to show that he praised Yazeed. They do this by only selectively producing extracts from his writings. Take a look at the full extract from Ibn Kathir and make up your own mind on what he thought of Yazeed:

'And Yazeed had some praiseworthy attributes such as mercy, kindness, eloquence, poetry, political astuteness and social etiquette. However he also had a concentration of carnal desires and would miss prayers sometimes and delay them most of the time. Imam Ahmad narrated from Abu Saeed Khudri that he heard the Prophet ﷺ say 'In the year 60 there will be caliphs after him who will lose the prayers and follow their desires and will soon be in the *Gayy* (valley of Hell).' (Al bidaaya wa Nihaaya)

This passage shows that Yazeed possessed the evil traits disliked by Islam. Some people only quote the first part of this passage and try to prove he was, according to Ibn Kathir, a man of mercy, kindness and bravery. However we must remember that these traits can also be found in non-Muslim rulers, in Islam what maters is one's relationship with Allah and with the Prophet ﷺ, to which the second part of this passage refers to.

3) Yazeed was a narrator of ahadith

Ibn Hajar Al Asqalaani writes:

> 'No narration of Yazeed is acceptable. Yahya bin Abdul Malik bin Abi Ganiyya who is one of the Thiqa narrators said that Nawfal bin Abi Aasab, who is a Thiqa narrator, narrates that he was once in the company of the pious caliph Umar bin Abdul Aziz when a man mentioned Yazeed and referred to him as Ameer ul Momineen, Umar bin Abdul Aziz protested 'You say Ameer ul Momineen Yazeed?!' and ordered he be whipped twenty times. I (Ibn Hajar) have mentioned Yazeed bin Ameer Muaawiya so that he can be distinguished from the Yazeed in Maraaseel Abu Dawud.'

4) Imam Husayn was not a companion

The reason some try to negate Imam Husayn's rank of companionship is to exclude him from the virtues and honours of companionship and so then be free to attack him.

Imam Husayn's rank of companionship is acknowledged by scholars such as Allaama Ibn Kathir and Imam Ahmad ibn Hanbal. Ibn Kathir writes about Imam Husayn:

> 'He was from the leaders of the Muslims and the Ulama Sahaba. He was also the son of the Prophet's ﷺ daughter, who was his most dearest daughter. He was an abid, zahid, brave and kind.' (Al Bidaaya wa Nihaaya)

This proves that for Ibn Kathir Imam Husayn was not just a companion but of the Ulama Sahaaba.

Hafiz Ibn Hajar Asqalaani writes:

> 'For some of them it is conditional that during the period of companionship they are mature, but this is rejected for it would exclude the likes of Hassan bin Ali and others from being companions. Imam Bukhari has declared *jazm* upon it (that they are companions) and it is also the statement of Imam Ahmad and the majority of the muhaditheen' (Fath ul Baari)

Some claim Imam Husayn was too young to be considered a companion. However the leading scholars reject this too; Khateeb Baghdaadi in Kifaaya tu'l Khateeb writes:

> 'Verily Imam Hassan bin Ali has narrated from the Prophet ﷺ and was born in the 2nd year of Hijrah.'

This quote makes Imam Hassan's age as 8 at the time of the Prophet's ﷺ passing away and Imam Husayn must thus have been seven years old. Other historians have stated that they were born in years 3 and 4 respectively. This would still make Imam Husayn over 6 years old. Even if he was five at the Prophet's ﷺ passing away every Muslim knows that the house in which he grew up was the treasure chest of knowledge and wisdom, its environment enlightened by the

Prophetic light and filled with the constant reminder of Allah and His Prophet's 🌺 teachings. In addition Imam Husayn was a special pearl of the Ahl ul Bait, who was showered with the specific bounties of the Prophet 🌺, and who had a physical and natural likeness with the Prophet's 🌺 character. To compare him to the other children of his age and say he was too young to know what was happening around him is a severe ignorance of his elevated status. The people of knowledge and wisdom know that in every time where there are ordinary circumstances there are always special and exceptional circumstances. If we were to look closely enough we could find such circumstances even today.

5) Yazeed had nothing to do with Imam Hassan's death

Yazeed was involved in the poisoning of Imam Husayns's elder brother Imam Hassan. Imam Suyooti writes:

> 'Imam Hassan died in Madeenah from poisoning. Yazeed had sent a secret message to Imam Hassan's wife Ja'da bint Ashat promising that if she poisoned Hassan he would marry her, so she did. After Imam Hassan's death she reminded Yazeed of his promise to which he responded 'I did not prefer you for my enemy (Hassan) so how can I prefer you for myself?!'

Shaykh Abu Ali Al Faadhl bin Hassan At Tibri in his book *A'laam ul Waraa'* writes:

> 'After the reconciliation between Imam Hassan and Ameer Muaawiya Imam Hassan left Kufa for Madeenah and resided there for 10 years. Then his wife Ja'da bint Ashat bin Qais Al Kund poisoned him. He remained ill for 40 days. Yazeed had enticed that woman by promising to pay her 100,000 Dhirhams and marrying her after Hassan's death. The woman did so i.e. she poisoned him. When Imam Hassan had passed away she reminded Yazeed of his promise to

which he responded 'We did not prefer you for our enemy (Hassan) so how can we prefer you for ourselves?!' (Nur ul Absaar)

The Aashiq ur Rasool Molaani Jaami writes :

'It is common knowledge that his wife Ja'da poisoned him on the say so of Yazeed bin Ameer Muaawiya.' (Shawaaid un Nubuwwah)

Shah Abdul Aziz Muhaddith Ad Dehlvi writes:

'The cause of Imam Hassan's death was his wife Ja'da bint Ash'at bin Qais poisoning him on the enticement of Yazeed bin Ameer Muaawiya. Yazeed had promised to marry her in return for this act. So she did it and Imam Hassan lay ill for 40 days before dying. Ja'da then sent a message to Yazeed reminding him of his promise and Yazeed responded 'I did not prefer you for my enemy (Hassan) so how can I prefer you for myself?!' Thus she became of those who lost in this and the next world and this is a clear loss.' (Sirr us Shahaadatain)

THE JIHAD OF CONSTANTINOPLE

Did Yazeed not lead the Jihad of Constantinople, and is he not because of that promised Paradise? And is the one who does not deem him of Paradise rejecting the Prophet's ﷺ hadith narrated in Bukhaari?

There is a hadith of the Prophet ﷺ narrated in Bukhaari in which he said:

> 'The first army from my 'Umma to fight in the city of Caesar will be forgiven.' (Bukhaari)

Those who present this hadith as evidence for Yazeed must remember that this is the statement of the Prophet ﷺ who had knowledge of all the events that were going to happen until the end of time. Look carefully; he did not say that every army that fought in the city of Caesar would be forgiven but specifically restricted it to the 'first army' i.e. only the first army would be forgiven, and Yazeed was never amongst the first army that fought in the city of Caesar: Allaama Ibn Atheer states:

> 'In the year 49, some say it was 50, Ameer Muaawiya sent a strong army to the cities of Rome with Sufyaan bin Oaf as it's

Ameer. He ordered his son Yazeed to also take part but he remained at home making excuses so Ameer Muaawiya did not send him. During this expedition the army was afflicted with severe hunger, thirst and illness, upon which Yazeed rejoiced with the following verses 'I do not care if fever and trouble has gripped them at the station of Farqoonda, especially when I am sat here with Umm Kulthum on a large cushion in a high chair'. Umm Kulthum was his wife. When these words reached Abu Sufyaan he swore that he would send Yazeed to Rome to fight under Sufyaan bin Oaf so that he too could face the difficulties the others faced.' (Ibn Atheer)

This passage proves a number of facts:

1) The first expedition to Rome was headed by Sufyaan bin Oaf and not Yazeed.

2) Yazeed was not amongst the first expedition, and the glad tiding and forgiveness is specific to the first army. Thus Yazeed is in no way the subject of it.

3) Yazeed had no sincere intention or desire to fight in the path of Allah. He tried many excuses in the face of Ameer Muaawiya's command and turned away from both Jihad and his father's order.

4) Yazeed had no sympathy for the Mujahideen of Islam and had no appreciation of their plight, their pain or their thirst and hunger. Indeed he even boasted of his indifference to their dying from thirst and hunger!

5) The state of his pleasure seeking was such that he openly said that he wanted and preferred the soft bedding and pillows and the company of Umm e Kulthoom.

6) He was only sent with the subsequent expedition as a punishment. Ameer Muaawiya vowed to send him as a punishment for his

poetry. Thus he did not perform Jihad in the path of Allah with sincerity but went forcibly.

7) Jihad is an ibaadah and sincerity is a pre-requisite of ibaadah. Without sincerity no act of ibaadah is worthy of acceptance and this narration makes it as clear as the day that Yazeed only took part in this jihad as a punishment. It was not with sincerity.

Imam ul Muhadditheen Imam Badr ud Deen Aini, the commentator of Sahih Bukhaari, wrote:

'It is said that Ameer Muaawiya sent an army under Sufyaan bin Oaf to Constantinople and it advanced through the cities victoriously. This army included Ibn Abbas, Ibn Umar, Ibn Zubayr and Abu Ayyub Ansaari. Abu Ayub died during this siege and was buried there. I say that it is clear that these great companions were under the leadership of Sufyaan bin Oaf. They were not under the leadership of Yazeed for he was not worthy of having such great companions under his command. Muhallab states that this narration is praise for Ameer Muaawiya for he was the first to begin naval expeditions and it is also praise for Yazeed who took part in the first jihad upon Constantinople. I ask how could this be praise for Yazeed when Yazeed's character and condition is very clear?! If you say that the Prophet ﷺ declared forgiveness for this army then I say that it does not mean that Yazeed cannot be excluded from this general rule by way of another rule. There is no disagreement amongst the Scholars that those within the rule of 'being forgiven' are only those who are worthy of being forgiven. If anyone of that army (later) becomes an apostate then undoubtedly he will not be part of that general rule. Thus it is clear that this glad tiding of forgiveness is only for those who are able to be forgiven.' (Umda t'ul Qaari)

Allaama Imam Qustalaani, the commentator of Bukhaari, writes below this hadith:

'From this hadith Muhallab has tried to prove the Caliphate of Yazeed and his being from the people of Jannah for he is amongst the generality of 'they are forgiven'. The answer to this (claim) is that this kind of statement is only made in support of the Banu Umayya and even if Yazeed is part of the generality of this hadith it does not mean that he cannot be specifically excluded through any other reason. This is because there is no disagreement in the fact that the Prophet's ﷺ statement 'they are forgiven' is conditional upon being worthy of forgiveness. Thus if someone after that battle became an apostate then he, with unanimity, will not be part of this glad tiding. Ibn Muneer has mentioned this and some of the ulama have performed La'na upon Yazeed, as Allaama Saadudeen Taftazaani mentioned in Shara Aqaaid' (Irshaad us Saari)

Ibn Hajar Asqalaani and Shaykh Ali bin Shaykh Ahmad have mentioned something similar, see Fath ul Baari and Siraaj ul Muneer.

This proves that this hadith of glad tiding in no way applies to Yazeed. There is a principle 'When there are several interpretations/possibilities, it cannot be used as proof' and as there are so many historical variations (possible different scenarios) of the Hadith of Constantinople one cannot use it as a proof. For example there is a hadith of the Prophet ﷺ 'Whoever recites *There is no god but Allah* will surely enter paradise.' After reciting this a person becomes of the people of Jannah. But will he remain from the people of Paradise if he only continues to utter this *kalima* verbally? Of course he will not if he refuses Zakah, Jihad and the finality of the Prophet ﷺ etc and commits heresy! Thus because of these specific rulings he will come out of the general rule of 'Whoever recites *There is no god but Allah* will surely enter paradise'. The reasoning behind this is that one does not become worthy of Jannah by simply reciting the kalima by tongue, one needs to believe and act upon all the requisites of that kalima, which include paying Zakah, undertaking jihad, believing in the finality of the Prophet ﷺ etc. To remain a believer it is necessary to recite this kalima with a true and sincere heart and remain steadfast upon it in all respects, or else he will become like the hypocrites whom Allah declared as liars and from the deepest echelons of hell. Similarly after the Jihad of Constantinople Yazeed, because of his actions, became deprived of the honour and rewards of the Jihad of Constantinople.

VIRTUES AND EXCELLENCES OF IMAM HUSAYN

The virtues, qualities, abilities and laudable deeds of Imam Husayn, the beloved of the Prophet ﷺ, the light of the eyes of Zahra Batool; the comfort of Ali, the contentment of Hassan's heart, the chief of the youth of Paradise, the cream of the Prophet's ﷺ Ahl ul bait, the chief of the Sa'daat, The Qibla of the needy, the leader of the mujaahideen, the Imam of the Muslimeen, the forbearer of the Arifeen, the imam of the Aashiqeen, the martyr of the plains of Karbala, our Chief, our Master and our Imam, salawaat and Salaam upon his grandfather, his father, his mother and his brother, may Allah be pleased with him, are countless. And why would they not be when his household was the treasure chest of virtue, blessing, goodness and perfection. Whatever blessing anyone has received has been as a result of the bestowment of this household.

In particular the Prophet's ﷺ statement 'Husayn is from me and I am from Husayn' reveals that he was the Prophet's ﷺ beloved and the refection of his perfections and qualities

Verse 1

Allah states {O Ahl ul Bait, Allah wishes only to remove pollution from you and to purify you with a thorough purification} (Al Ahzaab v33)

This verse is the foundation of the Ahl ul Bait's virtues. It begins with the term of *Hasr* (comprehensiveness) 'Inna maa', meaning that He, who is Qadeem, intended to keep them pure from all types of pollution and the verse ends with a *Mafhool Mutallaq* 'Tatheera' which denotes exaggeration and means that they attained perfect purity, extinguishing any notion that the verse could merely refer to symbolic purity. Furthermore the *tanween* upon Tatheera denotes honour and multiplicity meaning that it was not any ordinary purity but the best and highest order of purity.

This verse proves that Allah purified and freed (*munazza*) the Ahl ul Bait from all types of impurities and evils, whether in belief, deed or character and rendered them the highest rank and position of cleanliness of heart and good manners and purification of the apparent and hidden and thus making them distinct and superior over all others. Although after such purification they do not become Ma'soom (innocent) like the Prophet's ﷺ they do however become Mahfooz (protected). In light of authentic ahadith and reliable exegesis of the Quran Imam Husayn is without a doubt from the Ahl ul Bait and thus the *misdaaq* (subject) of this verse.

By accepting this verse of the Quran we must acknowledge that Imam Husayn's blessed heart was pure from the yearning of status and wealth or the desire of government and worldly position because such a condition is just the basic level of the heart's purity and cleanliness.

Verse 2

Allah states {'Say: 'Come! Let us call our sons and your sons, our wives and your wives, our selves and your selves, then let us humbly pray and invoke God's curse upon those who lie"} (Quran 3:61)

This blessed verse is known as the verse of Mubaahala. The Prophet ﷺ, with his beloved daughter Syeda Fatima, son-in-law Syeduna Ali and grandsons Imams Hassan and Husayn, arrived for a Mubaahala with the Christians of Najraan and pleaded 'O Allah this is my Ahl ul Bait' (as narrated by Muslim). When the Christian high priest saw their enlightened faces he warned his people:

'Verily I am looking at faces who if they ask Allah to move the mountains from their place Allah would do so through their supplication. Do not take part in a Mubaahala with them for you will be destroyed and no Christian will be left on the face of the Earth until Qiyaamah!' (Tafseer Kabeer, Tafseer Khaazin wa Mudaarik)

This verse reveals that as the subject of the term 'Our sons' Imam Husayn is the son of the Prophet ﷺ; Syeduna Usama bin Zaid states 'I saw the Prophet ﷺ with both Hassan and Husayn saying 'These two are my sons aswell as my daughter's sons, O Allah, I love them and so You too should love them and love whoever loves them.' (Tirmidhi)

Thus when it is proven from the Quran and Ahadith that he is the son of the Prophet ﷺ and a part of the Prophet ﷺ then the similarity in character and nature that a part of the Prophet ﷺ would have with the Prophet ﷺ himself was manifest in Imam Husayn perfectly.

Verse 3

{'Say (O Muhammad) I do not ask of you any reward for this (preaching) except to love my Qurba (kin)'}(As Shura v23)

Abdullah bin Abbas narrates that the Prophet ﷺ said:
'I ask for no reward from you for this except you love my kin and that you look after me in terms of my Ahl ul Bait and that you love them for my sake.' (Durr ul Manthoor)

Imam Ibn Munzar, Ibn Abi Haatim, Zarqaani and Ibn Mardwiya in their respective tafaaseers whilst Tibraani in Al Mujam Al Kabeer, Imam Suyooti in Ihyaa ul Mayyait bi Fadhaail il Ahl il Bait, narrate from Ibn Abbaas:

'When the verse 'Say (O Muhammad) No reward do I ask of you for this except to love my kin' was revealed the companions asked 'Yaa RasoolAllah, who are your kin who we must love?' He replied 'Ali, Fatima and their children.'

Imam Hassan in one of his sermons said:

'Whoever recognises me verily does recognise me, and for the one who does not know me I am Hassan bin Muhammad.' He then recited the verse '*Wattaba'tu Millata Abaai Ibraheem*' and said 'I am the son of the Al Basheer, I am the son of the An Nazeer,' and also added 'I am from the Ahl ul Bait whose love and friendship Allah has made obligatory upon you and about which the verse 'Say (O Muhammad) I do not ask of you any reward for this (preaching) except to love my kin' was revealed upon the Prophet ﷺ.' (As Sawaaiq ul Muharriqa; Al Mustadrak)

Abu Delam narrates that when Imam Zayn ul Abideen was brought to Damascus as a prisoner and made to stand in one place a local wretch said to him:

'Praise be to Allah who has killed you all and cut you at your roots and destroyed the perpetrators of fitna' (Ma'aaz Allah) Imam Zayn ul Abideen asked him 'Have you not read the verse 'Say (O Muhammad) I do not ask of you any reward for this (preaching) except to love my kin'?' He replied 'Yes'. (As Sawaaiq ul Muharriqa; Durr ul Manthoor)

When Amr bin Shuaib was asked the Tafseer of this verse he revealed:

'Qurba means the relatives of the Prophet ﷺ.' (Ibn Kathir)

It is in Sahih Bukhaari that Ibn Abbas was asked about the tafseer of this verse and Saeed bin Jubeer said it referred to the Ahl ul Bait of the Prophet ﷺ. On hearing this Ibn Abbas said:

'You have been hasty, for listen there was no tribe of the Quraysh that was not related to the Prophet ﷺ, so it means that there is a relation between you and I so keep this in mind and refrain from oppressing and hurting'.

The two statements of these great companions are not contradictory, the difference is that one is general whilst the other is specific. Ibn Abbas explained it in general terms whilst Ibn Jubeer did so in specific terms; Ibn Abbas took Qurba to mean the general relationship that existed between the Prophet ﷺ and the Quraysh, meaning the Quraysh should take account of that relationship and love him and not be his enemies. Whilst Ibn Jubeer took it in specific terms, meaning the relations of the Prophet ﷺ i.e love my family because of their relationship with me for loving them is in fact loving me.

Other mufassireen have taken this verse to mean that people should pay heed to their own relations and fulfil their rights. This tafseer is also based on generality for if one is required to love one's own relatives then the Prophet's ﷺ relatives have a greater right to be loved for he ﷺ said:

'No one of you can be a believer until I am more beloved to him than his own life, my offspring more beloved to him than his own offspring, my family more beloved to him than his own family and my person more beloved to him than his own person.' (Ibn Hibbaan, Bayhaqi in Shob ul Imaan; Nur ul Absaar)

The Prophet ﷺ also said:

> 'Teach your children three traits; love of your Prophet ﷺ, love of your Prophet's ﷺ family and the recitation of the Quran.' (Siraaj ul Muneer Shara Jaame us Sageer)

Verse 4

{'Verily Allah and His Angels send praise and blessings upon the Prophet ﷺ, O You who Believe, bless and salute the Prophet ﷺ with utmost laud and blessing'} (33:56)

Ka'b bin Ujza states:

> 'We asked the Prophet ﷺ 'Yaa Rasoolallah, we are aware of how to send salaam upon you, tell us how we should recite durood (blessings) upon you?' He replied 'Say 'O Allah send durood upon Muhammad and the family of Muhammad just as you sent durood upon Ibraheem and the family of Ibraheem. Verily you are the Hameed and the Majeed.' (Muslim, Mishkaat)

In another narration he said:

> 'Say 'O Allah send durood upon Muhammad and his wives and his offspring just as you sent durood upon Ibraheem, Verily you are the Hameed and the Majeed.' (Muslim)

Look closely at this, the companions did not ask the Prophet ﷺ how they should send durood upon him and his family, they only asked about durood upon him, but the Prophet ﷺ himself included his family with his durood, indeed he even declared the durood without durood upon his family as incomplete. The complete durood is only that which mentions the Prophet's ﷺ family with his mention. The

Prophet ﷺ said:

> 'Do not recite an incomplete durood upon me' and when he was asked 'What is an incomplete durood?' he explained 'That you say 'O Allah send durood upon Muhammad' and then stop, rather you should say 'O Allah send durood upon Muhammad and the family of Muhammad.' (Sawaaiq ul Muharriqa)

Abu Masud Ansaari states:

> 'The Prophet ﷺ said 'Whoever prays Salah and does not recite durood upon me and my family his salah will not be accepted.' (Daar Qutni)

As a result of this narration Imam Shafi'ee believes that reciting durood upon the Prophet ﷺ and his family is one of the waajibaat (compulsory acts) of the Tashahud. His couplet on this matter is well known:

> *'O Family of the Prophet ﷺ your love is an obligation from Allah in the Quran He sent to us*
> *It is sufficient for your great honour and prestige that whoever does not send blessings upon you has no prayer'*

In summary the Prophet's ﷺ adding of his family to his durood is a great proof of their honour and rank.

Verse 5
{'Salutations upon the Ilyaaseen'} (Quran 37:130)

Ibn Abbas in the tafseer of this verse states:

> 'We the family of Muhammad are the Ilyaaseen.' (Durr e Manthoor)

Some people have recited this verse as Salaam upon the Aal-e-YaaSeen which makes its meaning even clearer for one of the blessed names of the Prophet ﷺ is YaaSeen. As a result Allaama Ibn Hajar Al Shafi'ee Al Makki wrote:

> 'A group of the mufassireen have quoted from Ibn Abbas that the meaning of this verse is 'Salaam upon the family of Muhammad.'

Syed Abu Bakr bin Shuhaab ud Deen Al Husayni As Shaafi'ee writes:

> 'Naqqaash quotes Kalbi that Salaam(un) ala'l ilyaaseen means the family of Muhammad for Allah named him Yaa Seen just like Yaqub (was named) Israaeel'.

Verse 6

{'And all hold onto the rope of Allah and do not disperse.' } *(Quran 3:183)*

About this verse Imam Jafar Sadiq said;

> 'We (the Ahl ul Bait) are the Rope of Allah that Allah has mentioned in this verse.' (Sawaaiq ul Muharriqa)

Imam Shafi'ee confirms this in poetic form:

> *'And when I saw people going down the path (deen) of those who had drowned in the ocean and (of) ignorance*

> *With the name of Allah I boarded the boats of Salvation, who are the Ahl ul Bait of Mustafa, the Seal of the Messengers*

*And held onto Allah's rope, which is their love, as we have been
ordered to hold onto the rope.'*

Jaabir bin Abdullah narrates that he saw the Prophet ﷺ delivering a
sermon on the day of Arafa during the farewell Hajj whilst mounted
upon the she-camel Qiswa and he said;

> 'O people I leave in you that which if you hold onto you will
> not go astray; the Book of Allah and my offspring the Ahl ul
> Bait.' (Tirmidhi, Book of Manaaqib)

Zaid bin Arqam narrates that the Prophet ﷺ said;

> 'Verily I am leaving amongst you that which if you hold onto
> firmly you will not go astray after me, one of them is greater
> than the other; the Book of Allah is a lengthy rope from the
> Sky to the Earth; and my offspring, the Ahl ul Bait. These two
> will never separate from one another until they return to me
> at my fountain so look at how you deal with them after me.'
> (Tirmidhi; Mishkaat)

Verse 7

{And whoever undertakes a deed We will increase the deed} (Quran)

Abdullah bin Abbas in the tafseer of this verse states:

> 'This means the love of the family of Muhammad'. (Sawaaiq
> ul Muharriqa; Al Mustadrak)

Ibn Abbas states that the Prophet ﷺ said:

> 'People, love Allah for He bestows blessings upon you; love
> me for the sake of Allah's love and love my Ahl ul Bait for the
> sake of my love.' (Tirmidhi, Mishkaat)

Ali states that the Prophet ﷺ took the hand of Hassan and Husayn and said:

'Whoever loves me and loves these two and their mother (Syeda Fatima) and father (Syeduna Ali) will be with me at my Station on the day of Qiyaama.' (Tirmidhi, Baab ul Manaaqib)

This is the glad tiding that is more beneficial and precious than this whole world and everything in it! May Allah bless us with it! Abu Hurayra narrates that the Prophet ﷺ said:

'Whoever loved Hassan and Husayn has undoubtedly loved me and whoever has despised them has surely despised me.' (Ibn Majah, Al Mustadrak, Al bidaaya wa Nihaaya)

Salman Farsi narrates that he heard the Prophet ﷺ say:

'Hassan and Husayn are both my sons, whoever loves them loves me and whoever loves me is loved by Allah and whoever Allah loves He will enter into Jannah. And whoever despises these two despises me and whoever despises me is disliked by Allah and whoever Allah dislikes He will enter into Hell.' (Al Mustadrak Haakim)

Abu Saeed Khudri narrates that the Prophet ﷺ said:

'By the One in whose Hands is my life no one will have any malice towards the Ahl ul Bait except that he will be entered into Hell.' (Al Mustadrak of Haakim, Zarqaani ala'l Muwaahib; As Sawaaiq ul Muharriqa)

Abu Hurayra narrates that once the Prophet ﷺ came to us with Hassan on one shoulder and Husayn on the other and was kissing them both in turns. A man asked the Prophet ﷺ:

'Do you hold these two as beloved?' The Prophet ﷺ replied 'Whoever loves these two verily loves me and whoever dislikes these two verily dislikes me.' (Al Bidaaya wa Nihaaya)

Syeduna Barra narrates:

'The Prophet ﷺ saw Hassan and Husayn and supplicated 'O Allah I love them so you love them too.' (Tirmidhi)

Saad bin Malik narrates:

'I came to the Prophet ﷺ and Hassan and Husayn were playing on his blessed back. I said 'Yaa Rasoolallah, do you love both of them?' He said 'Why would I not love them?! They are my flowers in this world.' (Kanz ul Ammaal)

The people of Iraq asked Abdullah ibn Abbas about the issue of killing a fly or mosquito whilst in the state of ihram, in response he protested:

'The people of Iraq ask about the killing of a fly yet they killed the son of the Prophet's ﷺ daughter even though the Prophet ﷺ had said that both of them were his flowers in this world!?' (Bukhaari)

Zaid bin Abi Ziyaad narrates that once the Prophet ﷺ passed by Syeda Fatima's house and heard the sound of Imam Husayn crying and said:

'Daughter, do not let him cry, do you not know his crying pains me?!' (Tashreef ul Bashr, Nur ul Absaar)

Syeduna Usama bin Zaid narrates:

'One night I went to the Prophet ﷺ for a need and he came out holding something wrapped in a cloth. When I asked

'What is this?' he opened it to reveal Hassan and Husayn inside and said 'These are my sons and the sons of my daughter, (he then pleaded) O Allah, Surely I love them so You love them and love the one who loves them.' (Kanz ul Ammaal)

Abdullah states:

'The Prophet 鐊 was praying when Imams Hassan and Husayn arrived and when he went into *sajda* (prostration) they climbed onto his back. The people tried to stop them but when the Prophet 鐊 completed the prayer he said to the people 'These two are my sons, whoever loved them verily loved me.' (Al bidaaya wa Nihaaya)

Jaabir states:

'I went to the Prophet 鐊 and he was carrying Hassan and Husayn on his back and walking on all fours. I said 'How excellent is the conveyance' to which the Prophet 鐊 commented 'the riders too are excellent!' (Kanz ul Ammaal, Al Bidaaya wa Nihaaya)

Anas narrates that the Prophet 鐊 was asked:

'Which of the Ahl ul Bait do you love the most?' He replied 'Hassan and Husayn'; and he would say to Fatima 'Bring my two sons' and would smell them and hold them tight.' (Tirmidhi, Mishkaat)

Zaid bin Arqam narrates that the Prophet 鐊 said about Ali, Fatima, Hassan and Husayn:

'Whoever is at war with them I am at war with him and whoever is at peace with them I am at peace with him.' (Tirmidhi, Mishkaat, Al Bidaaya wa Nihaaya)

All these authentic ahadith prove the compulsion of loving the Ahl ul Bait and the prohibition of their enmity and hatred. This was the reason the esteemed companions, tabi'een and great Imams hugely respected and greatly honoured the Ahl ul Bait and had extreme love and affection for them.

Abu Bakr Siddiq said:

'By the One in whose hands is my life the Prophet's ﷺ relatives are more beloved to me than my own relatives.' (Bukhaari)

He also ordered:

'Safeguard Muhammad in his Ahl ul Bait.' (Bukhaari)

Meaning honour and respect Muhammad by honouring and respecting his Ahl ul Bait. Hudayfa narrates:

'I said to my mother 'I will pray Maghrib with the Prophet ﷺ and will ask him to supplicate for our forgiveness. Thus I attended the Prophet's ﷺ court and prayed Maghrib with him and then even prayed Isha with him. When the Prophet ﷺ left the masjid I followed him, on hearing my footsteps he said 'Are you Hudayfa? I replied 'Yes, Yaa Rasoolallah'. He then asked 'What is your need? may Allah forgive you and your mother. This is an angel that has never descended to the Earth before this night, (today) it sought its Lord's permission to present salaam upon me and give me the glad tiding that Fatima is the chief of the women of Jannah and Hassan and Husayn are the chiefs of the youth of paradise.' (Tirmidhi, Mishkaat)

Hudayfa al Yamaan states:

'One day we noticed the Prophet ﷺ very happy and asked

'Yaa Rasoolallah, today we are seeing you very happy and pleased.' The Prophet ﷺ said 'Why should I not be happy, Jibril has just come and informed me that Hassan and Husayn are the chiefs of the youth of Jannah and their father is better than them!' (Kanz ul Ammaal)

Ali states that the Prophet ﷺ said to Fatima Az Zahra:

'Are you not happy that you are the chief of the women of Jannah and your sons the chief of the youth of paradise?!' (Kanz ul Ammaal)

Abu Saeed narrates that the Prophet ﷺ said:

'Hassan and Husayn are the chiefs of the youth of Paradise.' (Al Bidaaya wa Nihaaya)

Jaabir narrates that the Prophet ﷺ said:

'Whoever would be pleased to see a man of Paradise (and in one narration, the chief of the youth of paradise) should look at Husayn bin Ali' (Ibn Hibbaan, Abu Ya'laa, Ibn Asaakir, Noor ul Absaar)

Ya'laa bin Murra narrates that the Prophet ﷺ said:

'Husayn is from me and I from Husayn, Allah loves whosoever loves Husayn and Husayn is a son from the sons.' (Tirmidhi, Mishkaat)

These statements of both Allah and His Prophet ﷺ clearly prove that Imam Husayn is Pure. He is the Prophet's ﷺ son, his flower and his beloved. He is also the chief of the youth of Paradise, loving him is compulsory for every Muslim and is the wealth of iman and the means to salvation. In truth love for him is not just love for Allah and His Prophet 🕮 but is the means of becoming beloved to Allah, whilst hatred of him is in reality hatred of Allah and His Prophet 🕮 and the means of entering Hell. The Prophet 🕮 has declared that the Quran and their connection is the means to remaining upon guidance and leaving them is the cause of misguidance.

As per these statements it is the Aqida (creed) of the Ahl us Sunnah wa'l Jamaat that the Ahl ul Bait's love is the stock of Iman, means to closeness of Allah and His Prophet 🕮 and the path to salvation. As a result of this status the elders of the Ahl us Sunnah wa'l Jamaat have included their blessed names in the Jumu'ah sermon so that this creed (aqida) can be disclosed and declared upon the pulpit and their love and devotion can be firmly established in the hearts of the Muslims.

Consequently anyone who criticises him, and attributes envy, hatred and desire of status and government to him and declares him a rebel, mischievous and troublemaking and declares his virtues mentioned in the Quran and hadith as mere imaginary, is without doubt outside the Ahl us Sunnah wa'l Jamaat, misguided, anathema and of Hell.

Remember that Creed *(Aqida) is* based upon the news given by the Quran and hadith and is not created from the selective information derived from the unattributed narrations found in the books of history. Our belief is upon Allah and His Prophet 🕮 and not upon the biased views of any historian.

History can be proven wrong, but the statements of Allah and His Prophet 🕮 cannot be wrong. Consequently all scholars are agreed that the historical viewpoints that contradict the Quran and ahadith are false and rejected. If we were to make our creed in line with history it would mean that Allah and His Prophet 🕮 were subject to the rules of history, thus rather than keep our Aqida in line with history, history must be kept in line with our Aqida

Furthermore those who distort historical sources through selective editing and manipulate and twist the meaning of those sources and pick and select sources to fit their views and impure motives, and then pass them off as 'research' and establish one's creed accordingly in direct contradiction of the clear sources of the Quran and Hadith are in nothing but ignorance and naivety.

Historical research is to consider all historical sources in their true light and meaning and establish the true picture of events. If however one takes the sources out of the context in which the historian presented them and tops and tails them to fit one's own distorted or prejudicial viewpoints then this is not historical research but a distortion of history.

Praise be to Allah for His favours that with the Prophet's ﷺ specific benevolence and kindness this sinner has been, for the pleasure of Allah and His Prophet ﷺ, able to provide well reasoned and evidenced answers to the questions raised so that they benefit the people of Imaan and are a source of guidance for the critics. I end with the supplication that my effort is accepted by the Ahl ul Bait of the Prophet ﷺ and that they intercede for me before the Prophet ﷺ and the Companions so that on the day of Qiyaamah the Prophet ﷺ becomes my Shaf'ee (intercessor).

Ameen
Muhammad Shafee Okaarvi